I0144892

The 9 Truths

Don't F*ck up your life!

Dr. Stephanie Aldrich

Disclaimer

Although the author and publisher have made every effort to ensure that the information in this e-book was correct at press time, the author and publisher do not assume and hereby disclaim any liability to any party for any loss, damage, or disruption caused by errors or omissions, whether such errors or omissions result from negligence, accident, or any other cause.

This e-book is not intended as a substitute for the financial advice of professional financial brokers, planners, and insurance agents.

This e-book is not intended as a substitute for the medical, marital, or spiritual advice of physicians, psychologists, counselors, therapists, and clergymen. The reader should regularly consult these professionals in matters relating to their physical and mental health, particularly concerning any symptoms that may require diagnosis or medical attention.

Copyright © 2023

By Stephanie Aldrich.

All Rights Reserved.

978-1-7333770-2-7

Dedication

To Noah and my future grandkids,

"How long are you going to wait before you demand the best for yourself?"– Epictetus

---

      That is one of my favorite quotes. It reminds me to not wait to do, be, and have what I want. You can live life if you go after it. Don't wait. Live it today! Today is all you have. Follow the 9 Truths, and you'll get there faster and easier than ever imagined!

Love,

Mom/Nee Nee

Table of Contents

Introduction

"You only live once, but if you do it right, once is enough." —Mae West

---

If you're older than 40, you didn't grow up in the Information Age. *You* were the remote control and had to get up and change the channel every time your dad wanted to watch something different. There was no internet. There were no cell phones. The phone I had growing up had a cord hooked to the wall. I was so happy when my dad installed a 20-foot cord so I could stretch the phone and talk to my friends in the bathroom.

We only had a few stations as our small township didn't have cable access until I was well into my high school years. Therefore, all of our wisdom came from two sources:

-Experience

-People we knew

That's it. It was either trying something to see if it worked or listening to your Uncle who tried it before and either succeeded with it or failed miserably. So Generation X learned to do things our way. We didn't want to rely on others; we just put our heads down and figured it out.

Even in the Information Age, we're (Generation X) still like that. Yes, we're more educated because we can learn anything from watching a YouTube video or a quick TikTok. But all in all, we're the same type of people. Learn something and get on with it. You either fail or succeed. If you fail, you try something different and do it again until you get a different result.

This book was written by combining my experience on The 9 Truths, and the wisdom shared with me by people I know or admire. I am writing this so that my future grandbabies can live well and with intention. I want them to make their own mistakes, not ones they should have learned to avoid from me. I don't want them to go backward. I want them to evolve and leapfrog to an unchartered territory where they can succeed, contribute, and grow.

None of these truths are new. You probably have heard of most or all of them. The question is, do you believe them? Do you follow them? Do you live by them?

And if not, why? Why would you intentionally not follow the wisdom tested over generations and generations of human history?

Your grandmother or uncle probably said something to you about them over dinner once, but you blew them off. "They're old," you may say to yourself. "They don't know what they're talking about in the 21st century. That doesn't apply to today." Unfortunately, you'd be wrong. Dead wrong. And I will prove it to you again and again throughout this book.

We all have a short time to live. Some live to be 100 but never really live their lives. Others live to only 30 but live intentionally and with vice and vigor. Which side of the coin do you want to be on? Do you want to make mistake after mistake and never find yourself ahead in life, living a mundane average of 75 years? Or do you want to get the 9 truths out of the way, plan your journey, and have the energy, money, and time to live an extraordinary life? It's a decision you can certainly make at any time, but why not make it when you're young? Why waste time when no one knows exactly how much time we have?

Why not leave all the cards out on the table? Why not strategize your hand, so you end up with a winning hand? Why not play a game that you're an expert in and can win easily and quickly? That's what this book is all about. That's what you can learn by reading this book. Learn what is real about the world we all live in, and skip the rest. No matter when you read this book, these 9 truths are timeless. They are true no matter what religion you practice. They are true no matter what socioeconomic class you find yourself in. They are true no matter your sex. That's why they are called the truth.

Dictionary.com defines the word truth as "The quality or state of being true. That which is true or in accordance with fact or reality. A fact or belief that is accepted as true."

The truth is law. Everyone has agreed that the law is real and that we as a society should live by them. Gravity has been agreed upon as a fact. Mathematics has been agreed upon as fact. The seasons have been agreed upon as factual or true.

The truths I talk about in this book are:

- Compounding

- Mindset and perception

- What is Enough

- Karma

- Simplicity

- Intention

- Health- mental, physical, and spiritual

- People and relationships

- The Flat Ass Rules

No one can deny that these ideas and concepts are facts. No matter what religion you believe or don't believe, these 9 Laws of the human condition transcend time and space. Everyone deals with all 9 of them at some point in their lives. Some work *with* the truths and allow them to guide them to live their dream lives. Others go *against* them and find that things don't usually work out for them along the way. If these truths are learned early and used frequently, anyone can live a long and fruitful life full of love, friendships, money, and adventure.

And isn't that what most people want? I don't know many people that love to be in debt, be in a 450-pound body, and have no family or friends. Most people don't want to live that kind of life, but too many people, unfortunately, live that way. This book is worth writing if I can help just one person skip that line and journey into a life of prosperity, love, and fun. Dive in and remember, you only live once (as far as we know), so make it count and live your life by The 9 Truths!

Chapter 1

The Compound Effect

"Compound interest is the eighth wonder of the world. He who understands it earns it. He who doesn't, pays it." –Unknown

---

Dictionary.com defines compounding as "To increase the value of something over time." The compounding effect can be seen with investments such as compounding interest. It can be seen in goal setting. Each step along the path to our targets can combine and give us the results we're working toward. Compounding can also have negative effects, such as in weight gain. Suppose there's a surplus of calories over time. In that case, those calories are often converted and stored into fat for the body to use at a later time. Everything we do over the course of our lives can compound and add positively or negatively to our lives.

Darren Hardy described this phenomenon in his book, *The Compound Effect – Jumpstart Your Income,*

Your Life, Your Success. He found that making small intelligent decisions over time can result in extraordinary measures. These small decisions need to be aligned with what's important to us. When we align what's important to us and make decisions that align with those values, our journey can lead us straight to our goals.

In today's society, we want instant gratification. We take a pill that will magically help us lose 20 pounds. We click on Amazon and order something that can be delivered to our house later that day. We watch our *On Demand* shows whenever and wherever we choose. We stop by the fast food drive-thru because we're hungry. We turn on the faucet, and water comes out so we can wash our hands.

We're so caught up with our instant lives that we forget to focus on how we can use the present moment to build momentum toward our future goals. We can allow our focus and attention to stray from things that don't matter to us and represent our core values. Distracting actions and thoughts can cloud our minds and waste our resources.

We are taught to "think big" and "reach for the stars," only to barely survive and reach average levels of success. The average American earns around $68,000 per year. The most common size of clothing for a woman is size 14. The average American reads four books a year. These are hardly successful numbers, but statistics don't lie.

Why are we taught to "think big" only to realize mediocre results?

David Brooks, the writer of *The Atlantic,* describes the downfall of nations as the failure of their citizens to trust their institutions, their moral convictions, and each other. It seems that we as a society can veer off track and lose our focus on the things that have given us the success we've enjoyed.

This distrust doesn't happen overnight. It happens over time through incremental changes to policies and behaviors. One change may not seem detrimental at the time it was made, but it could have disastrous effects over time. Incremental changes compound and create large overall effects when given enough time to experience them.

In 1994, the North American Free Trade Agreement, otherwise known as NAFTA, was implemented. It was designed to phase out agricultural products, textiles, and automobile tariffs. It was supposed to promote trade between the United States, Canada, and Mexico. The agreement meant a trade-free zone for the three countries. However, the effects of this agreement were different than their intention.

NAFTA did help the U.S. GDP (gross national product) but, in turn, helped to drive American jobs to Mexico in favor of cheaper labor, helping to contribute to inflation. The agreement also increased the less-than-beneficial trade deficit, where American imports grew more than their exports.

American jobs were leaving the country. Foreign dependence on our resources decreased while *our* dependence on foreign resources increased. Unemployment numbers increased to almost 6%, according to Statista.com. Certain industries, such as farming and automotive, were deeply affected.

An agreement to help everyone win ended up hurting the very people it was supposed to help. Since there were lower restrictions on trade, big corporations moved factories and left their workers in the dust. My father, who worked for Delphi, an automotive business supplying General Motors with car parts, went belly up and shut down, leaving my father without a job. This hit home hard since my father wasn't of retirement age but in his 50s. Luckily, he had a side hustle that he built and turned into a thriving local business that could sustain our family after Delphi closed.

That's the compound effect in motion. One agreement led to thousands of other decisions that affected millions of people's lives throughout our country. Sometimes we think a thought or action will end up giving us a positive result. But in reality, it causes many devastating side effects in its wake.

What about the drug Celebrex? Celebrex was approved by the FDA in 2004 to help with tenderness, inflammation, stiffness, and pain caused by rheumatoid arthritis. A year later, Pfizer was warned to take the drug off the market as increased risks of heart attack and stroke were found in patients taking the drug.

Celebrex was supposed to help with one thing and exacerbated another in turn. That's compounding in full effect. One thing leads to another and builds on itself.

What about the American obsession with losing weight and getting in shape? Any athletic trainer will tell you that getting your body into form requires many different steps over a certain amount of time. Professional athletes use their off-season to make improvements to their results. They may focus on their nutrition, physique, and a certain statistic measured during their performance.

In 1989, Michael Jordan, arguably the world's greatest basketball player of all time, hired Tim Grover, a well-known athletic trainer, to help with his strength and endurance training. Michael knew that his body was getting beat up and that if he was to peak during the playoff season, he would need to be strong enough to handle the grinding 80-plus game season.

Tim wasn't concerned with making Michael quicker, stronger, or faster because that could make him more susceptible to injury. Tim wanted to make Michael less susceptible to injuries, especially to his legs and ankles, so he could not only jump higher and run faster but also endure the grueling schedule without being on the injured list.

Tim started with conditioning and strength exercises that built a foundation for all of Michael's fancier skills. Tim knew Michael could remain fresh and energetic in the fourth quarter if his conditioning was superior to all other athletes. This would help him take over the last moments and create the amazing last-minute game-winning shots he later became known for. This is a key example of the compound effect.

We all create a strong foundation of fundamental skills that can lead to more complex results. Professional athletes know this, and anyone else can do this. It takes dedication to the fundamental skill sets and the power and strength needed to deliver those fundamental skill sets with expertise.

This foundational mindset doesn't have to be just in athletics. It can also be demonstrated in other areas of our lives. Let's look at business in general. For any business to succeed, some fundamental principles must be obeyed.

One of those principles is sales. No one loves to be in sales, but if you work for any corporation anywhere on Earth, you're all in the sales game one way or another. Whether you work directly with customers or as an executive, someone somewhere must be convinced that your ideas are legit and should be used and implemented.

Being great at sales and communication doesn't happen overnight. Yes, some people are charismatic and naturally a *people* person. But trying to create a want and a need for your product, service, or idea is a fundamental skill set that needs to be learned, practiced, and mastered if we are to make a successful career in a corporation.

This foundation starts with communication with the customer or executive. Asking them about their needs is one of the most important things any sales person can do. If you know what their main problem is, you can then determine if your product, service, or idea can solve it. Then, and only then, can you use your communication skills to bridge the gap between your product, service, or idea with the solution to their problem.

This fundamental skill requires lots of practice and discipline to master. Knowing how to gain a customer's attention and keeping it is involved. People tend to put up their defensive guard against sales people because they feel that salespeople, in general, try to persuade them into purchasing unwanted things.

A professional salesman doesn't use persuasion tactics at all. Instead, a professional salesman simply makes their customers aware of their problems and how they can solve them with the salesman's product, service, or idea.

A professional salesman doesn't allow negativity, objections, or complaints to get in the way of helping their customers. Their main mission is to help their customers and, in turn, are rewarded for their efforts. But to become a highly paid sales professional, the sales process fundamentals must be mastered, which takes practice, patience, and lots of time.

Some say that it takes 10,000 hours to become a master at a skill set. Malcolm Gladwell popularized the 10,000 rule in his book, *Outliers.* An important factor that distinguishes a professional from an amateur is not only how much time they spend honing their skills to professional status but also what areas of that fundamental skill they should focus their attention on.

In other words, how good their teacher was.

Michael Jordan was already a great athlete. No one can deny that. But Tim Grover didn't focus on the skills that Michael already had but focused on the skills that he lacked that would bolster those other skills. He knew that the focus should be on stamina, energy, and endurance. Hence, Michael could perform the other skill sets he already possessed and perform them at an extraordinary level.

The sales game is similar. If you start by becoming an expert at handling objections and complaints, you can become great at demonstrating and closing the sales process. One leads to the other. Mastering one fundamental area of focus can lead to success in other areas. They build or compound on one another.

How can we use the compound effect in other areas of our life, such as our financial life? Have you ever heard of the term *compound interest*? Most people have heard this term but haven't realized its powerful effect on their finances. This is an exemplary example of how the compound effect works.

Theodore Johnson worked for UPS yet never made more than $14,000 per year. Throughout his career, Theodore saved 20% of his income and invested it in UPS stock until he retired in 1952. By that time, he had accumulated about $700,000 worth of stock. Over the course of the next 30 years, the stock grew to over $70 million. Yes, $70 million.

Ronald Read was a janitor and gas station attendant who amassed an $8 million fortune when he died at the age of 92 in 2014. He always invested in the stock market, choosing blue-chip investments such as Procter and Gamble and General Electric as main staples. That's the compounding effect at its prime.

According to Brian Preston from *The Money Guy* podcast, a 20-year-old only needs to save and invest $95.40

per month with a 10% return, such as the S and P 500 index fund that averaged over 10% over the past 40 years, to reach millionaire status by age 65. Consistent incremental investments over time can build wealth. Money multiplies. Then that money multiplies and accumulates. And so on and so forth.

Time is on our side when it comes to compound interest. Unfortunately, most of us are on the other compound interest spectrum, debt. Compound interest can do wonders for our wealth accumulation when consistent deliberate investing occurs over our working lifetimes. At the same time, it can also have very negative, consequential effects on the negative side when we use debt.

76% of Americans live paycheck to paycheck. Why? Consumer debt and payment plans. According to Marketwatch.com, Americans owe over $790 billion in credit card debt. That's over $5300 per American. Mortgages are even worse at $9.5 trillion. That's a lot of payments going out of our paychecks every month.

An average 30-year mortgage of a $250,000 home is around $1564.17 at a 3.25% interest rate and will pay $127,517.12 in interest over those 30 years. So the house you bought at $250,000 will end up costing you

$352,517.12 in the end, let alone all the improvements you'll make over the course of your lifetime. Will you get that money back when it's time to sell? Probably not. So the banks win instead of you.

Everything is available for purchase on payment plans nowadays, and many of us want to buy things instantly but don't have immediate cash. So we use payment plans to satisfy our desires. That's why our payments are eating up our paychecks. These payment plans charge interest on things we bought in the past and negate our desires for things in the present and the future. We're paying for our past discretions now and in the future. It's a very sad and avoidable thing. But we must change our mindset and behaviors when it comes to compounding interest.

Something that can create wealth very easily over time can also obliterate it in the same manner. This is why radio personality and YouTube star Dave Ramsey has had a long-lasting career. With over 10,000 advertisements being seen on an average day in America, no wonder we have become an instant gratification consumerist nation.

Marketers make us feel inadequate if we don't have their product. *If you have this problem, click on the link below. If you want to be this, buy now before the quantities run out.* It's a never-ending cycle of psychological warfare. Marketers now use psychological tactics to make us aware of our flaws and convince us that we could be superior if we use their products and services. They make us feel bad about ourselves or the situation that we're in. It's a very evil and profitable strategy that we must be aware of and avoid at all costs!

Realize that these marketers don't know you, nor do they have your best intentions at heart. Their only objective is to sell you stuff. When you buy their stuff, they get more companies to pay them to market more stuff to you. That's it—psychology for sale. And the marketers bought it and repackaged it to take advantage of you, your emotions, and your wallets.

Then there are social media posts with all of the beautiful rich people pushing items on you. They make their lives look perfect on Instagram, only to be broke and desperate for their next gig in real life. Influencers span the internet, becoming today's product endorsers preying on our desires for a better life.

Social media and marketers have completely duped our society and used psychological warfare to do it. I've dabbled in it myself. In 2020, I took a course on advertising on Facebook pushing supplements and other digital products. These people were making millions of dollars a month pushing these drugs without proof of effectiveness. I finally learned the system and made over $80,000 in sales in one month, earning a cool $40,000 in commission. In one month. Think about that for a minute. All I did was create eye-catching illustrations with vague messaging to create that inadequacy that would make the person click on my link and buy the supplement. The people who taught me how to do this knew all the buttons to hit, and I hit them all. It was easy, and it worked. No, I didn't use any of the supplements. No, I didn't know if any of them worked. I didn't care. I just wanted to pay my house off, and I used that money to help me accomplish my goal.

I would still be doing it today if Apple hadn't stepped in and decreased the retargeting capabilities of Facebook. The next month, my sales went back to 0. I used that money to put on my mortgage to pay it off sooner. No harm, no foul. And I don't feel guilty about it, either. If these people who bought this supplement were too stupid to research its effectiveness or ineffectiveness, then why should I care? I was marketing to them, not advising proven medical treatment. It was easy and sad all at the same time.

What sales and marketing tactics have we all fallen for in the past? *Buy now and have payments for as low as $125 a month. Buy now; limited supplies available. Sale ends Tuesday; buy now.* The list goes on and on.

Urgency. Inadequacy. Solving problems we didn't even know we had. These are all scare tactics that salespeople and marketers use to get us to buy. We need to build that thick skin that people without consumer debt have to resist the temptations to purchase things they can't afford or don't need.

Dan Kennedy built a multi-million dollar business writing copy using persuasion tactics for some of the world's biggest companies, including Guthy-Renker, Tony Robbins, and Proactiv. His purpose was to enter the customer's head and ask the questions that the customer was already asking and answer them in his sales copy. *Are you embarrassed? Do you feel tired all the time? Will this work? Can I do this? Will it work for me?* He could hear the conversation in the customer's head, address the objections swirling around, and make the customer take action. He enticed people with the product's features and benefits and created urgency with product promotions that created the customer's desire to solve their problems. He was a master at it, and companies paid him millions of dollars to help them persuade their customers to want and buy their products.

His tactics were simple and effective. *Give them what they want, and they will continue to buy from you.* We all tend to be suspicious when it comes to sales tactics. We've all been duped by a shady salesman who promised us the moon and then failed to deliver it. But in the end, it was our own desire that duped us. Why do we want to change ourselves this much? Why are we so unhappy that we think someone's product or service we've never heard of before can swoop in and solve our problems? We've got to start waking up and becoming aware that all the advertising and promotions surrounding us have one main strategy: to take our money. When we realize this, we'll think twice about parting with it. This is surely the compounding effect in prime action. They want to wear us down. They want us to feel desperate and victimized, looking for a hero to come and rescue us.

Have you ever calculated how long it took you to earn that amount of money? You spent 8 hours making $50 an hour to earn that $400. Then the government takes out 1/3, leaving you with $280.   Do you need a new iPhone? Does your old one still work? What about your car? You just got done paying for it; it's now yours outright. Why do you need to purchase another one so soon after paying this one off? Why not have a few more payment-free years and use that money to pay off other debt or invest in your retirement fund?

But I only pay $30 a month, so surely I can afford a new phone. Sure, you can afford the payment, but what happens when your iPhone gets smashed or lost, and you have to buy another one? It took three years to pay off the last one, and now you're paying another $30 a month to purchase a new one that will be outdated before you pay off the other two. See the vicious cycle?

What if you got into an accident in your new car? Did you know that cars depreciate 40% within the first three years? That means your car is already losing value as soon as you take that car off the lot. This also means if your brand new car gets totaled, your insurance company won't write you a check for what you owe on your loan, and you'll actually still owe the bank money on this trashed car.

Dave Ramsey and even Brian Preston from *The Money Guy* podcast say to pay for everything in cash and buy used if you can or use it until it breaks down. This includes cars, clothes, and electronics. Brian does have a plan if you can't buy a car in cash. He recommends putting 20% down on it, not financing anything more than three years, and not having your payments be more than your investments and 8% of your take-home pay. These guidelines help you stay in control of the depreciation game.

What about good old credit cards? Credit cards are a prime example of compound interest working against you. The average credit card interest is 18%, according to wallethub.com. 18 percent! That means buying $5000 worth of stuff on a credit card at 18% interest will take you 47 months (almost four years) at $150 a month to pay it off. And if you do pay it off, you will have paid an extra $1983 in interest. So that $5000 actually cost you $6983. Ouch!

Today, we buy houses on 30-year fixed mortgages. According to Fool.com, the median cost of a house in America is $374,900. Now, I know that depends on where you live, but let's say you buy a home for $250,000 at 4% for 30 years. Your monthly payment will be $1194. That doesn't include property taxes, closing costs, and home insurance. That's just the mortgage and interest. When you're done with the payments, you will have paid over $326,000- an extra half of the house! *But I can afford the payment.* Sure, but that payment is stealing $126,000 from you in the meantime. Remember, compound interest can work *for* you, not *against* you. If you took that extra $126,000 ($350 over 360 months and invested it at a conservative 8%, you would end up with over $492,000! You earned almost five times your money! And $350 isn't a lot of money. What if you didn't have a car or credit card payment of $800 a month? That $800 a month invested at a conservative 8% for 30 years would end up being over $1.1 million! Now that's using the compound effect for your own use!

For some reason, Americans today are in the habit of buying things on payment plans. *If I can afford the payment, I can afford the thing.* What we don't realize is the true cost of these items. If we keep buying things, we don't have any money left to upgrade items. We don't have any money left to go on vacations. We don't have any money left to fix things. We don't have any money to save. We don't have any money to invest in making even more money. In other words, *we* aren't in control of our money; the *payments* are.

Look at your bank statement right now. How many checks did you have to write to other companies for stuff that you bought? Yes, we all have utilities, food, transportation, and homes we must have. But do we need to spend every dollar we have on those things and the stuff that goes along with them? What if something goes wrong? What if we get sick and can't work? What if another Covid situation happens and we lose our job? Can we get out of the obligations that we have? Or do we own all of our stuff outright with enough cash reserves and investments to cover us if something happens?

"It's gonna rain. Dave, be more positive. I'm positive it's gonna rain."- Dave Ramsey

---

I know I have talked a lot about Dave Ramsey and Brian Preston in this chapter. I have binge-watched every episode they've done on YouTube over the past couple of years, and they have taught me the true power of the compound effect on my money. You can use the compound effect in so many ways. For your health. For your mental state and attitude. For your generosity. For your finances. For your security. For your success. It only takes one decision: use the compound effect for you and not against you. The banks know how to use it. Companies know how to use it. Marketers know how to use it. Unfortunately for us, they're using it against us instead of trying to help us. Don't be a victim of it. Use it to gain health. Use it to gain skill sets that can advance you in your career. Use it to become financially stable and independent of the payment mentality that has plagued many of us.

Be weird. Be different. Call your own shots. Live independently of big corporations and lousy manipulative marketers. Let your neighbor play victim to their empty promises and their shallow lies. Control *your* desires for more stuff and allow the compound effect to create the life you've always wanted.

Chapter 2

Mindset & Perception

"If you change the way you look at things,
the things you look at change." -Dr. Wayne
Dyer

What Dr. Dyer is talking about is perception. We may look at some old scrap metal and think to ourselves, *This is just junk.* But this same scrap metal is valuable to someone who recycles scrap metal or an artist that uses scrap metal to create sculptures to sell. The scrap metal is just scrap metal. It's an object that doesn't change. But it's our opinion or perception of it that forms the connection we have with it.

According to Dictionary.com, perception is "a single unified awareness derived from sensory processes while a stimulus is present." Our senses pick up a stimulus from our environment, and our mind then creates an understanding of that stimulus. That understanding could be useful, not useful, harmful, necessary, or unnecessary to our overall well-being.

Remember that saying as a kid, " Sticks and stones can break my bones, but words will never hurt me?" This is all about perception. You may say something nasty to someone, but they don't react. You may say the same thing to someone else, and they react by punching you in the mouth. It's all about perception, how someone forms an opinion about that word, phrase, or object, and how it can affect their life. Some people take words seriously. Some don't. Some people are very opinionated and want the whole world to know their opinion, and some aren't. Some people learn a new concept and completely change their mind or belief about that thing, while others are set in their ways and never change.

It's all about their perception of the world and the ideas we humans have formed. In *Hamlet*, Shakespeare wrote, "It's neither good nor bad, but thinking makes it so." Perception goes hand in hand with comparison. You may think it's cold outside, but is it really cold? If you compare the temperature to that of Florida or during Summertime, then, yes, it's colder. But what if you lived in Canada? That same temperature may be warmer than that of our friends from up north. Our perception must go hand in hand with a comparison of some sort to be accurate.

Comparison

"Comparison is the thief of joy." –
Theodore Roosevelt

In 1954 psychologist Leon Festinger developed an idea called "The Social Comparison Theory." His research, along with others, showed that as much as 10% of our daily thoughts involve comparisons. According to these studies, some people use the comparisons to improve themselves and change their perceptions about what they think is true. In contrast, others use the comparisons to experience depression or guilt for what they think they lack.

Interestingly, we tend to compare ourselves to others worse off than us if we're trying to motivate ourselves to improve. Then we compare ourselves to others who are better than us when we're devaluing our efforts. So comparison is tied to our perception or opinion about something, and our perception is directly tied to the comparison we use to form our opinion.

What comes first? The chicken or the egg? You may argue that the egg must come first because most species on earth start their life form during a zygote phase. But who made the zygote? Some may use the Adam and Eve theory that believes there must have been a male and female chicken that got together to form the egg. Either way makes sense, but no one knows for sure because none of us were around to see it with our own eyes.

Perception

"All things are subject to interpretation. Whichever interpretation prevails at a given time is a function of power and not truth."-Friedrich Nietzsche

The next question is, how are you perceiving your life? Who and what are you comparing it to? Are you fat? Are you rich? Are you smart? Compared to who? You may be the first one in your family to graduate with a college degree. If you compare yourself to your other friends and family with no degree, you're probably feeling accomplished and proud. If you compare your physical education degree, where you'll only make $40,000 a year, with another person who earned a medical degree making $400,000 a year, you may not feel so proud or accomplished. It's how you look at things, right? It's perception by comparison.

What we don't understand about perception by comparison is that the comparison we use to understand the world around us is always skewed. We may think that all millionaires inherited their money because we grew up in a neighborhood where the average household income never exceeded $30,000. It's nearly impossible mathematically to become a millionaire on $30,000 in today's society. So I agree that it would seem daunting to save and invest enough money to compound over time to become a millionaire. But that's only the perception of the millionaire idea, not the reality.

Brian Preston's team from *The Money Guy* Podcast did the math on this and showed that if a person who was 20 saved $95 a month at a 10% return would reach millionaire status by the age of 65. $95! That's less than most monthly cell phone bills. $95 a month. So perception or misunderstanding, in this case, creates a very powerful and false perception of what it takes to become a millionaire in today's society. $1,000,000 probably won't get you that far, considering how much inflation over your lifetime will eat away at that pot of money. Okay, so how much would that 20-year-old need to save a month to build a nest egg of $3,000,000? According to Brian, a 20-year-old would only need to invest $286 a month at a 10% rate of return to accumulate three million dollars. If you did the 4% withdrawal rate on three million dollars, that's a cool $120,000 a year. Considering the average household income in the United States, according to the US Census Bureau, is just over $65,000, you can throw out the perception that you can't become a millionaire by using compounding interest over time.

If you're 35, you only have to save $452 a month to reach that same three million dollar status. It's the equivalent of maxing out your Roth IRA every year. That's all! But you must start and be consistent over time to allow your money to make money off the interest. What most people with a poverty mentality forget about or don't use is the magic of consistency over time. But they grew up in a poor neighborhood where nobody learned about these things. So the same neighborhood will produce the same mentality generation after generation.

Most people don't grow up in poverty because they want to. They grow up in poverty because they don't know they can live differently. It's the old saying, "They don't know what they don't know." Poor neighborhoods base their beliefs on lack and not abundance. They don't value education. They don't value hard work. They don't value ambition. It's sad but true. The belief that to be wealthy, you must have been born with a silver spoon in your mouth is simply an excuse and lack of knowledge. It's ignorance at its best. But to change that mentality, the perception by comparison game must stop.

We've gotten so trapped in keeping up with the Joneses and comparing ourselves to others that we've lost touch with what's really important. How do you perceive yourself? Are you proud of who you are? Are you kind to others? Are you a good teammate? Do you help others with your products and services? Do you spend time with your family and friends? Do you take care of those around you? Are you saving and investing for the future? Do you spend your money conservatively? These are the things that matter. Not what fancy vacation your friend just went on and showed on Instagram. Most of the posts on Facebook and Instagram are perfect instances. You don't see the ten shots they had to take before they got the not-so-perfect shot of their family with the kids and the dog. All you see is the perfect shot, and compare it with your own life circumstances.

The best way to start improving yourself is not to step on someone else to do it but rather stop comparing yourself to others. Everyone is different. Everyone has been blessed with different talents, circumstances, and physical capabilities. Embrace what you've been given and use it to the best ability.

The Greek Philosopher Epictetus, born around 50 AD, said in *Enchiridion*, "Control your perceptions. Direct your actions properly. Willingly accept what's outside your control." He also wrote, " Some things are in our control, while others are not. We control our opinion, choice, desire, aversion, and in a word, everything of our own doing. We don't control our body, property, reputation, position, and in a word, everything not of our own doing."

Comparison and perception are two things we spend a lot of our time and energy on when, in fact, these two things can be completely eliminated from our lives. Why spend time and energy comparing yourself to an Olympic athlete when you're paralyzed from the waist down due to a car accident? You can't change the fact that you won't be able to walk again, so why waste valuable time and energy wishing things were different? Yes, you can vicariously live through someone, but why? We all have unique qualities and abilities that we should spend every waking moment perfecting and sharing with others.

We've all been given a certain deck of cards to play with. Why not play the best game we can with what we have? This doesn't mean we can't win the game with a lousy pair of twos. This means we must play the game strategically with what abilities and qualities we have. We all need each other. We all have products and services that can help others who lack those products and services. I'm not the best at wiring up my house. Why waste my time learning how to become an electrician when I can hire someone who already knows how to do it? I'm a dentist. That's what I have been trained to do. Other people pay me to take care of their oral health. You don't see others watching YouTube videos about dentistry and trying to do it themselves, do you? At least, I hope not!

In *Thou Shall Prosper*, Rabbi Daniel Lapin wrote, "You will just need to find your own way to see the beauty and nobility in how you earn your living. The rule is that people seldom excel at any occupation that, deep down, they consider unworthy. God wants you to love other people. You do so through service. And He rewards you for it."

In the long run, it's not about *comparing* yourself to others, but it's about *helping* others live a better life; in return, they help you live one too. Tearing someone down so you can benefit isn't the right way to live. Feeling bad about yourself because someone has what you want isn't either. We must take a look at our own lives and what abilities and talents we were born with and improve them to the point that others want and need our help too.

Many people in this world play the victim. They think they can't do anything important because of their skin color, the neighborhood where they grew up, or their family circumstances. They blame the government, family, and environment for their shortcomings. Again, they compare themselves and their lot in life to others. What they are missing is their own responsibility in their circumstances and the belief that they can change things.

"If you're born into poverty, it's not your fault. If you stay in poverty, it is."– Bill Gates

---

Most people don't understand that we are in control of our lives. We control how we think and feel about the world around us. Yes, some people live in poverty. Yes, some people live under harsh government control. But no one can take away your free will. No one can take away your right to be happy and live the best life you can. Yes, sometimes certain *rules* can make it more difficult to do that. But everyone needs to take responsibility for their thoughts, actions, and omissions no matter where they start in life.

Viktor Frankl was a psychologist who survived the Nazi concentration camps during World War II that took away his family. He said, "Everything can be taken from a man but one thing: the last of human freedoms—to choose one's attitude in any given set of circumstances, to choose one's own way." He observed the characteristics of those that survived those terrible, barbaric circumstances and noticed they, including himself, did so not from luck or opportunity but from attitude. From meaning. From hope. The hope of a better life. Surviving into the future to live their full purpose. Helping those less fortunate than ourselves.

An easy way to get your mind from comparing yourself to those more fortunate is to think of those around you that are less fortunate and do something in your power to help them. When you're focused on helping someone better their life, you'll be less concerned about comparing yours to someone else. This is because you're being of service and focusing on things you can control. You can control your thoughts, emotions, and actions. When you're helping others, you show your gratitude for living a meaningful life, no matter what circumstances you may face.

This is where mindset kicks in. Attitude. Perseverance. Fortitude. Creativity. Awareness. All of us have the ability to create the life we want, no matter where we live on Earth. It all starts in our minds with imagination and creativity. When we stop comparing ourselves to others and creating negative opinions about everything, that frees up our resources (time, energy, and money) to live our best life. Think about that for a moment. If you're not worried about Facebook or Instagram and spend your free time working on your health or your side hustle that you hope to build up to full-time status, how much progress will you achieve toward your best life?

What does that best life entail? In one word: *Freedom.* Freedom of thought. Freedom of ambition and creativity. Freedom of finances. Freedom from debt. Freedom of health. Freedom of time management.

Freedom to travel. Freedom to learn. Freedom to grow and become better. Freedom of relationships. Freedom of activity. Freedom of speech. Freedom of belief. Freedom of results. Total freedom.

Today, we live in an instant gratification society. Fast food. Movies on Demand. Buy now, pay later on four easy payments. With the internet, we can have our groceries delivered to us today. We can purchase anything we want from anywhere in the world with a push of a button. What we fail to realize is that instant gratification doesn't equal freedom. Instant gratification usually means enslavement. We become obligated to that thing we must have. We must dress a certain way. We must act a certain way. We must have certain things. All of the instant gratification items come with a cost. It's the cost of giving up our financial freedom. We work 40 hours (at least) a week to earn money that flies out the door to other people as we try to pay them back for the item we *had to have*. We give up our time and freedom to work extra hours to afford the dance lessons that our four-year-old daughter wants. The same daughter who trips over her two feet, we're sacrificing our time and energy to pay for those lessons.

Our attitude, which is nothing more than our feelings and opinions about life, is that this type of life is normal. That's the American dream. To own a house, a car, a white picket fence, to have a spouse and two kids. That was the old mentality of the American dream. The new American dream is to buy everything and anything I want and to take antidepressants because my life still sucks. Even though I own everything I could ever want, I'm still miserable. Why?

You're miserable not because you owe everyone something but because of your entitled attitude. The attitude in today's America is that of entitlement. The Millennials have deemed themselves the *entitlement generation*. They think they are entitled to the American dream because they are here on Earth, not because they earned it. Just because you're an American doesn't mean you're entitled to anything but freedom. But *you* must work toward that freedom and not expect to have anything you want on shere[AS1] merit. This is another example of the perception by comparison game.

You can't compare yourself when you're young and just starting your career with someone with twenty years of experience. I challenge any young dentist out there that thinks they can outproduce me in the amount of time that I work. I've been running my own business for over twenty years, and if I'm ever challenged by someone, I'll smoke them where they stand! Experience outweighs entitlement any day of the week. The experience helps to form the belief in what's possible. It's the experience that allows freedom to prevail.

When you want everything now, you miss out on the experience of working for it. You miss the decision-making skills created when you decide if this is important and worth your time, energy, or money to get it. You miss the sacrifice and hard work that went into the achievement. You miss out on the person you become on the journey.

"Setting goals is not about what you get. It's about who you become in the process." –Bob Proctor, star of the movie *The Secret*

Accomplishing a goal, losing weight, or changing your environment is not about the endpoint but how the process changed you during it. What habits did you need to change to succeed? What beliefs were shattered once you achieved that goal?

Once you achieve a goal or change a bad habit that's been keeping you stuck for years, your mindset starts to shift. You start looking around at other areas of your life that you can change and improve. Your attitude about your future starts to change. You start to help others around you improve their lives. You start to believe that the old story you told yourself about living by other people's rules doesn't apply to your new life anymore. It's your mindset that starts to shift.

It really starts with your mindset. Your thoughts. Your feelings. Your beliefs. Do you believe you're in control of your life, or do you play victim to its circumstances? Do you have discipline and follow through with what it takes to achieve your goal, or do you shy away from the challenge and believe that everyone and everything is against you? Do you believe that the sky's the limit to your imagination and creativity, or do you feel you're stuck because of who you are and where you came from?

It's all about the Yin and Yang of life. You either live on the bright side or the dark side. It really boils down to another *Star Wars* theme. "There is no try; there is only to do," as Yoda said. It's about making the most of the cards that we're dealt. It's about how we can use our God-given talents to help other people. Maybe we're not the biggest or strongest people in our neighborhood, but maybe we can sing. Maybe we're not the smartest in our family, but we can write.

The whole point of this chapter is to make you look inside yourself. Your mind. Your heart. Your soul. What's really in there? What type of person do you want to be? What do you want to be remembered for?

I've been reading a lot of Stoic philosophy, and many think that the Stoics are quite non-emotional and mean. On the contrary, I have found out that they were very insightful and always thought about their place in society and how they could help their community. But one thing that struck me as poignant was that no matter what they said, what insight they came up with, or what wealth and power they had, all of them got older and died.

Yep, no matter what, they all died. And no matter what, all of us will die too! I know it's a little crass to say it. But unless you realize that at any time, you could die and decide to live every day to its fullest, you will end up wasting your days on frivolous attitudes and things.

One of my friends received news that her boyfriend had cancer. This man was the same age as me, in better health than me, but I found out he was sick. It made me realize, yet again, that my life is also running out. My life, like yours, is a ticking clock no one knows when the alarm will go off. My question to myself is, how will I use the time I have been given? And that's my question to you? Will you waste your time, energy, and money on things that don't really matter? Will you fight with other people? Will you eat crappy food so your body becomes ill and you can't take care of your family and responsibilities? Will you stay angry at the world for not giving you the opportunities you think you deserve? Will you hold grudges? Will you be selfish? Will you lie, cheat, and steal from others? What type of person do you really want to be, and how will you spend the time you have on Earth, making sure you are that person?

I know, deep stuff, huh? Phew, let's take a breath right now and step back from philosophy for a moment and close our eyes and feel for a moment and ask ourselves, what type of person do I want to be?

Whatever thought comes into your head first, that's the first idea you can run with to create your improved mindset and attitude. If you want to be more generous, start thinking of ways you can do that. If you want to be in better shape, go to the gym right now and slowly start running or lifting weights. If you want to make more money, think of skills you can learn to make that happen. Do you need to minimize spending? Do you need to earn more? Do you need to save more?

When you have a thought when your mind is quiet, usually this thought is not coming from your mind. It's coming from your soul. It's coming from your spirit connected to everyone and everything in this Universe. But most of us block out these inner thoughts and feelings because we're too caught up with our environment and playing the comparison game. Stop it! If you don't, you'll regret wasting your life on stupid shit that doesn't matter.

That's why I write. It's my soul coming through in these words. Before I write, I always close my eyes and think about what I want to bring to my family and others who read these words. What wisdom can I give to them? What insights about life can I share with them that could help them in difficult situations?

I've noticed or, better yet, realized from reading philosophy that dated back to the Jesus era that the people who lived thousands of years ago are no different than you and I. They have the same core values. They love their families. They defend their beliefs. They help one another. They love. They cry. They have sex. And they create rules to live by. These rules are all directed inward, not outward, as they know that the only person they can control is themselves. That's what the 9 truths are about.

Knowing what is real and what isn't. Knowing what's important in life and what's not. Living your life to its fullest and never sacrificing your wants and dreams unless it means harming others to get them.

But it all starts inward. It all starts from spirit radiating thoughts into our minds. Can you be quiet enough to listen? Can you forget your false beliefs and narratives about your circumstances and open your mind to these truths? We all come from the same spirit, and we'll all circle back to find it again. But how long will it take you to free yourself from your false beliefs and narratives? How long will it take for you to damn everything and everyone that's ever told you that you couldn't do something and go for it? Will you ever get it? Will you free yourself and live the way you want without comparing yourself to others? Will you live to your fullest and share your talents with others?

Close your eyes and go with your gut instincts. Close your eyes and imagine your future and where you want to be. Close your eyes and imagine the person you want to become. Then open your eyes and move into action. Move into the action you instinctively know is in the right direction toward your dreams.

Never allow anyone or anything to get in your way. Never quit. Become resilient to obstacles. Become resilient to the naysayers around you. It's your mindset and your belief in yourself that will allow you to succeed. Your motivation and ambition will open up new ideas and thoughts to use. Use this creativity, your mind, and your will to go where you never thought you'd go. Be the person you want to be, not who you think others want you to be. You can do anything. You can be anyone you want to be. You can live with dignity, success, wealth, strength, and ferocity. Anyone can. At least, that's my plan in my life. Will you join me? Or will you fall back into the popular story of playing the victim and allowing others to control your story? It's up to you. It's always been up to you, and it will always be up to you. Close your eyes and imagine what you want and what kind of person you want to become, then go for it. You can do it! You must do it!

Don't Try, Train

"Successful people do what unsuccessful people are not willing to do. Don't wish it were easier, wish you were better."– Jim Rohn

On a Dave Ramsey podcast, someone said a very interesting thing, "Successful people do consistently what other people do occasionally." Successful people set their mindset and beliefs not only to the future but to the present. They figure out what they need to do to live the way they want. They learn new strategies. They find new mentors. They change the things they need to change to go in the direction they want. They spend money, energy, and time to train. They don't *try*. They train. Trying never achieves consistent results. Training does. Trying is an attempt to change with minimal commitment. Trying doesn't require a lot of resources. Training does.

Think of your professional athlete. They don't *try* to improve their stats. They train. They hire strength coaches to build their muscle tone, strength, and endurance so they can play at their peak condition at all times. They practice fundamentals every day. They don't do it because they love the simple drills but to perfect them. They watch their competition to learn new strategies they can use for their own gains. They hire personal chefs to create a diet that not only keeps their bodies strong and healthy but can also help heal themselves during a tough season or during a period of injury.

Training isn't as simple as practicing something every day to improve. Training is about strategically practicing the skills that matter. Training brings every aspect of winning and victory together into one path. And training can help you and me reach our dreams and inspirations. But it needs to start with training, not trying, and certainly not comparing.

Training for you and I could include a new skill set that could get us a promotion or a new job and give us the increased income we need to pay off debt and invest for our futures. Training could include reading philosophy or metaphysics and learning how to use our thoughts to create positive momentum in our lives. Training may demand us to create a budget and learn how we can control our money instead of our money controlling us. Training could include hiring a health coach to help us get into shape and learn about proper nutrition.

Training takes time. There will certainly be obstacles that get in the way that can get us off track. We can't allow that to happen. If we eat something we shouldn't, the next meal, we get back on track with our proper eating. Training will take time. Everyone is busy. Everyone has families, jobs, and hobbies. But there's always time to train. There's always time to do the things that matter. That may be meditation. That may be cooking so we can follow our diet. That may be sitting down, checking our finances, and having a weekly family meeting about our budget. That may be family time. There's always time to train.

Training costs money. That may mean we need to spend money to hire a personal trainer to get us into shape and learn how to build muscle. That may mean a class we need to take to improve our marketing skills. That may mean equipment for our hobby that we want to spend more time enjoying. That may mean an extra job to get out of debt or put away in our children's college fund.

Training also will take some energy. We will need to move our bodies to create the tone and shape we want. We will need to go to the class and mentally focus our attention on learning the new skill. We will need to plan where our money is going and prioritize its use.

Training will use it all. It will take sacrifice. It will take endurance. It will cause us to be intentional with our resources. We will have to prioritize where we allocate our resources. We will have to change the normal habits that have gotten us thus far in our life journey. We will sweat. We will cry. We will become frustrated at times. We will miss things. We will be tired. We will feel stressed. But in the end, if we continue to train, we will find victory. We will find the goals we've been training for and smash them. We will collect our medals. We will persevere. We will win. We will get a new job. We will earn the money we deserve. We will become debt free. We will take the vacations we want. We will have the healthy, strong, sexy body we want. We will spend time with our families. We will live an abundant life. We will have fun and be happy.

That's what training, not trying, can do for you. Set your mind to accomplish something and put in motion the steps you need to take to accomplish your goal. Use your resources. Sacrifice a little time, energy, and money today for a better tomorrow. Believe that the effort you're putting in today will multiply your rewards in the future. Improve yourself because you want a better life, not because you're comparing it to someone else. That's what training will do for you. That's what living intentionally will do for you. Start today. Start right now.

Figure out what major things you want to change in your life right now.

Take out a sheet of paper and write down everything you want. Every place you want to visit. The person who you want to become. How you want to contribute to the world. Write it all out. Then find the one thing that you want to go after today. What's the one thing that will get you fired up? The one thing that will make a big difference in your world? The one thing that will take a lot of resources to accomplish but will reward you tenfold for its accomplishment. That's the one thing you should go after. That's the one thing you can start with because if you can become that one thing, the rest of your list will shortly follow.

It all starts with your mindset and your belief system. It all starts with the desire to do something different, start something new, and become someone else. If you're thinking differently, don't you think you'll start acting differently? You bet! You'll start making different decisions and taking different actions, giving you different results. But that doesn't include comparison. That doesn't include anxiety and doubt. That doesn't include a lack of focus.

Anyone that's ever done anything important has a clear plan and makes decisions that carry out that plan. They don't stray from the plan. They don't piddle away their resources. They use their resources to carry out the plan. Their time, energy, and money all go toward carrying out their plan. Sometimes, they need to pivot if the plan isn't going according to their blueprint. This is okay. But they keep their end goal in mind and take steps that get them closer and closer to their goal.

You can do the same thing. *Successful* people aren't more special than you or me. They aren't smarter, better looking, or more creative. But they create a plan and stick to the plan. They have persistence. They have guts. They have faith. They work hard, very hard. They believe that what they do will succeed. They believe everyone will benefit from their accomplishments and keep pushing for more. But it all starts with a clear vision. A positive and creative mindset. A concentrated focus on improvement and innovation.

Use your resources to accomplish something important! It doesn't have to be Earth-changing. It could be community-changing. It could be family-changing. It could be life-changing. We can always do something to improve ourselves, our families, and our communities.

Create the vision of how you want your life and environment to become, and then use your resources to create this reality.

Start with yourself and see how far you can take it. Educate yourself and start acting like the successful person you want to become. "Fake it until you make it!" By "faking it," you're throwing your thoughts and actions into the world you want. After some time and experience in this new world, you'll realize that you are that new person. You are living the new life you want. You are accomplishing the goals you've set. You are that new, improved person.

But it all starts with your thoughts, beliefs, and persistence. Start today! Don't wait! You can't take the next step tomorrow if you don't take the first step today. No matter how big or small, take the first step today!

Chapter 3

Enough

"Be content with what you have; rejoice in the way things are. When you realize there is nothing lacking, the whole world belongs to you."-Lao Tzu

---

According to Dictionary.com, the word enough means "Adequate for the want or need; sufficient for the purpose or to satisfy desire." Today, Americans grow up wanting more. We are pushed in school to get better grades. We want to buy new things constantly. We want instant gratification often. Marketers tease us with the latest and greatest gadgets that will somehow make our lives better and more meaningful.

The question is- when is enough enough?

The Buddha said we all strive for happiness due to the "fever of unsatisfied longing." We live for more. We crave better. We work hard to get ahead. We save our money to buy new and better things. We want our children to have all the things we didn't have growing up. We work for 40 years, save enough to retire, and realize that we don't know what to do for the rest of our lives. And for what?

When is enough enough?

What is adequate for you may not be adequate for me. What marketing messages influence me may not influence you. Most of the time, we crave more because of something missing in our lives and spirits. Maybe we grew up in a poor, tough neighborhood and do everything we can to pay for things that show others that we are special and don't want to go backward in our lives. Sometimes we don't have enough love growing up, and our careers and behaviors surround us with loving people and circumstances. Maybe we were chubby, and we got into fitness to feel proud of our appearance. There are always hidden motivators that form our beliefs and drive our actions.

But at some point, satisfaction must be obtained. A positive self-image must be formed. Confidence and worthiness must be held if someone is to be enough in life. You must ask the question, "When will you be happy?" When is enough enough?

My mid-life crisis was this- I worked so many hours- studied, and opened my own practice with hundreds of thousands of dollars in debt. I crawled my way out of it and became debt free. I renovated a beautiful house. I have a great husband and son. What does it all mean? I help thousands of people with their health every year. I make a good living. I travel when I can. I eat well. I have fun with my friends. What does it all mean? Why am I not satisfied?

Because I haven't defined what enough is in my life. At some point, you will meet your goals. You will achieve that insurmountable want that you've worked for for years. And when you get it, what will you feel? Not much. Because something inside of you will ask, is this it? Is this what I've spent my resources (time, energy, and money) trying to achieve? You'll find in the end that it really didn't matter to you. It really didn't make you a better person. It really didn't affect your life. It really didn't matter to anyone else around you, either. When you come to that moment when you've realized that maybe you're wasting your life on pursuing more; more money, more fame, more prestige, more physical items. Then you'll start to pursue different things in your life. Like meaning. Like generosity. Like love and compassion for others. Like traveling to distant lands. Like using your talents, wealth, and prestige to help others and not for selfish reasons. Then you will finally realize what enough is.

The famous comedian Jim Carrey said, " I think everybody should get rich and famous and do everything they ever dreamed of so they can see that it's not the answer."

So what *is* the answer?

What is our ultimate quest in life? I certainly don't have the wisdom or knowledge to answer that question, and I don't think it's the same for everyone. You will have to know what's enough for you. You'll have to figure out what makes you happy. Not everyone can write. Not everyone is strong. Not everyone can solve physics problems. But everyone has a talent that they can share with the world.

They may be strong athletes. They may be able to use words in a way to change people's minds. They may be able to paint, draw, and create art that allows people to escape a new reality. Everyone has a talent. Everyone has creativity, imagination, and the will to finish a job that's started. Everyone is enough in this world. It doesn't really matter where you were born, how much money you have, or what you look like. What matters is what you do with your life. What matters is who you help or inspire through your thoughts, words, and actions. How will you inspire the world? How will you persevere when times are tough? How will you find your purpose in life? You'll do that by pursuing your talent and knowing that you truly are enough, just the way you are.

Your Cage

"If you're trapped in a cage, you don't want to start being grateful for the protection of the bars. You need to be grateful that there are gaps in between them so you can see what's on the other side."– Beth Kempton

---

Isn't that a relief? I've given you the key to your own cage. You can't be free if you don't know you're bound. You can't be free if you're always looking ahead without realizing you can go in a different direction. You can't be free if you're constantly feeling that you need to be better than you are. Comparing yourself to others.

Living someone else's vision of what life is supposed to be. Is that what you really want? Is that how you want to live?

I never realized this until I started writing at 44. It took me many decades to realize that I was blind to reality. I had built a life that I didn't recognize, that wasn't true to me. And instead of doing something destructive or crazy, I decided to change some things about myself and what I wanted for my life.

I started reading philosophy. I started pursuing my writing passion. I cut down on work and structured my dental practice in a way that I could still make the same amount of money but in a third less time. I started eating better. I started traveling and having more fun with my husband, child, and friends. I became intentional with how I used my resources- my time, energy, and money. I got out of debt. I started to control my life and how I wanted to spend my remaining years. I learned about minimalism and realized that my grandparents lived this way their whole lives, and that's how they enjoyed retiring early and seeing the world. I realized that I could help people with not only my dentistry but also my words. I learned that I could start other companies and pursue other interests without sacrificing the people I loved or my time freedom. It took me a long time to figure this stuff out, but I had to ask myself when is enough enough? At 49, I finally found my answer, and I'm living enough right now.

What is enough for you? Maybe you want to pursue a career that allows you to live a laptop lifestyle of freedom and travel. Maybe you want to stay home and raise a family. Maybe you want to work in a non-profit charity and help others. Maybe you want to accumulate a lot of wealth by selling your ideas. Whatever you choose to do with your life, you should also choose a point at which you say, "This is enough." "When I reach this point, this is enough for me." "When I do this, it's enough." "If this happens, that's enough."

Throughout this book, different themes of minimalism and simplicity, taking control of your health and mindset, and taking actions that give you the desired results have come up. Everything we do robs us of our resources. When we're young, we think that the world is our oyster and that anything is possible. So we make certain choices in our daily lives that lead us down our life path. Then we wake up in our forties and wonder how we got to the point in our path that we are on. It happens to all of us. At some point, we look up from the weeds and wonder where we are, if we like it, or better yet, if we can change it.

The good news in all of this is that anything can be changed. We can change our finances. We can change our health. We can change how we view things and the people we allow to influence our opinions. We are all in control of our lives, and we can choose the point that we want to stop pursuing certain things and look around to smell the roses, so to speak.

Our mindset and beliefs help shape our actions and how we form our goals. At some point, we must realize the importance of the goals we're chasing. Do they really matter? Are they just a means to an end, or will they truly make a difference in our lives?

We're told that energy is neither created nor destroyed. All the energy that there is is here in different forms. We can manifest anything we truly desire if we take the right action toward the goal. But we must ask ourselves when we are done with the rat race. At some point, we must face the "truth" that we have believed in our entire lives and ask if that truth is real, if it's what we truly want, and if it's something we really want to manifest. This takes an awareness of our present circumstances and a change in our mindset that we've discussed in previous chapters.

I grew up in a little township in Ohio. My family actually founded the town in 1805 after Ohio became a state. My father was a mechanical engineer, and my mom was a housewife. We were on a tight budget, but my mom always saved for things that mattered to us and somehow seemed to make it all work.

I always wanted to help people and go into medicine. That led me to dentistry, where I racked up over $178,000 in student loans. Then I bought a practice and equipment, which amounted to another $450,000 more. Over the next twenty years, I'd scrap and build my practice to what it is today. I was making good money but was feeling the typical burnout in my mid-forties. I realized that I didn't really care about helping people anymore. I really wanted to help myself. I started reading and taking any self-help course I could find. This led to philosophy and creating the practice I wanted, which meant I could practice a few days a week and still have enough time and energy to pursue working on myself and my desires.

I look at the course of my life and ask if it was worth all the sacrifice and hard work I've put in over the past two decades. I can honestly say it wasn't. It's sad to say this, but it's true. I'm tied to my practice. I can't live a laptop lifestyle and live in Rome if I want. I can't go to work when I feel like it, as most people can't. I have appointments with people that dictate the time they want their dentistry done. I love my house and all the renovations I've done. But I could certainly live more frugally and simply in something smaller somewhere else.

I've lived my whole life in Ohio. But I hate the cold weather and would love to live somewhere during the winter. Unfortunately, I can't because I've spent so much money paying my debt that I haven't accumulated enough in savings and investments to live from its dividends.

So I'm stuck.

And I ask myself all of the time, was it worth it? At what point did I go past knowing when enough was enough? And that's where my focus, my attention, has shifted. I'm now only interested in things that I either love or will get me closer to financial independence.

You will come to this point too. It may be in your twenties as you're traveling with the Peace Corps and see how you can truly be happy with a simple life. You may find yourself in your thirties going through a divorce and find out that you could live the laptop lifestyle and pursue your hobby of photography because you're not pinned down to your old married life anymore. You may find yourself in your sixties and widowed with a stash of money ready for you to knock things off your bucket list.

No matter what age or stage of life you find yourself, you will have to make the decision when your enough has been met. Most of us aren't taught to think this way. We're taught to strive for more and more. We're taught to get better and better. To reach for the stars. To be the best we can be. But when do we reach this *state* of being the best? When do we take some time to live the life we're truly meant to live?

Self Image

"He who knows that enough is enough will always have enough"- Lao Tzu

---

I think the first place to start is with our own self-talk. Our own self-image. What are we saying to ourselves? What do we believe is true about ourselves?

Do we think we're too fat? Too thin? Do we live in a bad neighborhood and figure there's no way out? Are we not smart enough? Or too smart? Are we klutzy or always late? Are we flakey with our commitments or too unorganized to care? Are we always broke and depressed or stressed out and wealthy? Do we see the glass half empty or half full?

How do we see ourselves? How do others see us? It's not about comparison with others. It's about looking at ourselves and our attitudes, beliefs, and actions that we have and take and how they affect our lives and those that live around us.

Do we believe we can do anything? Or do we believe we can do nothing because of our unique circumstances? Do we argue with other people because we *want* to be right or because we actually *are* right? Are we skeptical of other people because of *their* actions or *our* actions?

The way we talk to ourselves matters. How we see ourselves matters, not necessarily to others but to ourselves. In Chapter 2, we talked about mindset and how it affects everything we do. Our self-image is based on our beliefs about the world and how we see ourselves in it. Do we think that nothing we do will help? Then, of course, we won't ever do anything that helps. Do we think we can never get that thing because of where we come from?

Then, of course, we can never get that thing because of where we come from.

It's a true dichotomy. What you say and think about yourself is *always* true. If you *think* you can do something, of course, you can do it. You'll find the resources and the way to do it. If you *don't* think you can do it, you'll never put in the effort and creativity to find the way to accomplish that goal.

How you look at things really does matter. How you look at yourself really does matter. How you visualize your future matters. How you value your worth matters. In America, why are so many people depressed? It's not that our country has more chemically inadequate people than any other country. So why do we medicate ourselves with drugs, alcohol, and food? It's because of our self-image.

We don't see that our lives really matter to the world. We don't take pride in what we do, what we have, or how we do things. We've become numb to the fact that we can improve ourselves and our communities. We've lost the fact that we live in the best nations on Earth. We've forgotten that we can live the American dream. We've lost the knowledge that we have talents and skills that others don't possess. We've lost the nerve to care.

We've lost the ability to feel important. To feel unique. To feel loved. We've lost the sense of when enough is enough for us.

We splurge on junk food. We waste our money on stupid gadgets and trinkets that have no value and need to be upgraded on a continuous basis because we see our friends doing the same. We sit on our butts and watch all the Netflix series, becoming disheartened when all of them run out. Why do we do this? Why are we wasting our lives in this manner?

Because of our self image.

For some reason, the majority of us settle. The majority of us don't care to improve. The majority of us have decided that their enough is average and mediocre. It's in our DNA to look for improvement, grow, and obtain better skills. But of course, there needs to be a cut-off point in the improvement. We've become lazy and complacent in our lives. We've become entitled and unwilling to take chances to grow and contribute to society.

The stresses of the modern age outweigh the need to climb the corporate ladder to success. We need to ensure that our self-image, no matter how much we earn, how much we weigh, and how much stuff we accumulate, is enough to start with. Then whatever else we accomplish during our lives is a bonus and icing on the cake (which is the best part.)

Expectations

"Blessed is he who expects nothing, for he shall never be disappointed." -Alexander Pope

Another idea that can totally derail our success, growth, and our formation of fulfillment and enough is our expectations. Most of the time, our expectations are not our own but derived from other people. Our families expect us to be a certain type of person, get a degree, and act a certain way. The community we live in expects us to contribute in a certain way, provide certain services to its members, and engage in complimentary social activities. The place we work expects us to finish certain aspects of projects, create certain plans, and move the business's mission forward.

It seems like everyone expects us to do certain things, and we can lose ourselves in those expectations.

What expectations do we have for ourselves? What do we want? Where do we want to spend our resources? What are our long-term goals for ourselves, our families, and our careers? What about our health? What about our finances?

If we live in a certain neighborhood, do you think there will be certain expectations on how we look, what car we drive, and what country club we belong to? Yep. If we are in grad school, do you think there will be certain expectations on what subjects and skills we learn, how we answer questions, and how to secure our tuition money? Yep. If we're trying to get into shape for a marathon, do you think there will be certain expectations on how we train, eat, and pace ourselves? Of course.

But are these expectations in alignment with our goals? Are these expectations ones that can push us to the next step? Are these expectations even ours? When we can define what enough is in every aspect of our life, we can then acknowledge which expectations align with our lives and which ones don't. Which expectations encourage us and our self-image, and which ones don't.

Wants versus Needs

"You can't always get what you want, but if you try sometimes, well, you might find you get what you need"- The Rolling Stones

What's enough for you in your house? What about in your bank account? How about in your closet? How big is your house? What brand is your car? How old is your phone? We are bombarded daily with thousands of marketing messages that tell us we should want more. Better. To upgrade. But are these marketing messages triggering our wants or our needs?

There are really only three physical needs: food/water, shelter, and clothes. That's all we need to survive. We don't even *need* clothes, but we wouldn't get anything done if we were running around naked all the time. But I included them in this list for our purpose.

Marketers know that they can tempt us into wanting their product or service by exposing our insecurities about ourselves and our environment. *Don't you want this cool phone? Don't you want to relax on the beach for a week and eat and drink as much as you want? Wouldn't you look great in this new car? You deserve it!*

I'm not saying that you can't have anything or everything you want. Because you can. What I'm asking you is, how much is enough for you? How messy do you want your closet? How much money do you want to owe the dealership on that SUV? How many years do you want to be in debt over some new boots and clothes?

When you decide what enough is, you'll find that you'll have exactly what you need and a little bit of what you want. When you decide what enough is, you throw the power of decision back in your corner. You can rationalize a purchase instead of buying it on impulse. You can become an informed buyer instead of being persuaded by peer pressure. You can live intentionally because you know what makes you happy and what doesn't. And if it doesn't, you don't waste your resources on those things.

When you finally realize that you've improved your health, got great relationships, and got enough stuff to have fun with, you can enjoy what defining enough truly means.

That's freedom.

Freedom from the rat race. Freedom from stress. Freedom from living your life on someone else's time schedule. Freedom from owing institutions money. Freedom to live your life how you see fit. Freedom to be happy.

"The ultimate failure is achievement without fulfillment."–Tony Robbins

---

Have you achieved everything you've wanted to achieve? Have you traveled? Have you had fun with the people that matter to you? Have you kept your body in shape? Have you saved and invested your resources for the future? If you haven't, create that "bucket list" right now and work on crossing the things off that matter to you. Things that you want to do, be, and accomplish with your life. You only go around once in this particular time and body that you're in. Why not make it an adventure? Why not make it the best life you can live?

How many people do you know or have heard of that had reached a pinnacle of success only to fall off the pedestal and die or dive into a drug frenzy, destroying everything they had worked so hard and diligently for?

Why? They were on top of their game, the best of the best. Why did they fall? Because they achieved their goals without being fulfilled by them. They didn't define what enough was for them and their life. They may have allowed their self-image (I'm not good enough), others' expectations of them (you should be the best), and their ego's wants (I want that Maserati because I can buy it, not because I need it) to control their thoughts and actions.

When you can define your goals, when enough is enough, and decide what your needs truly are, you can enjoy the freedom and fulfillment your life has in store for you.

Our minds and bodies know when enough is enough. Cholecystokinin is a neurochemical released in the body to tell your brain that it's full and that you shouldn't eat anymore. But how often have you ignored that feeling because you were eating your favorite meal or forced to clean your plate and not waste anything? I'm sure many times. Think of Thanksgiving. We gather for a big meal and to spend time with our families and loved ones, only to overstuff ourselves with food. How did that make you feel? Tired? Lethargic? Bloated?

What about going on a shopping spree? You got a bonus, and your favorite thing to do is to buy new clothes, so instead of paying off your credit card, saving for a rainy day, or using that money to invest, you spend it all on some new clothes and shoes. Did you really need all of those new items when your closet is full of clothes with tags on them that you've never worn?

We can get a dopamine and serotonin rush when we buy something new. It's a reward for our hard work. According to Healthline.com, dopamine and serotonin effects on the body can last up to 90 days! That's three months! That's a long time to feel that pleasure, that hit of adrenaline, that feeling of satisfaction from buying something new.

The problem with all of this is that it does eventually wear off. Then we seek to have that feeling again. What about that new car smell? Of course, that only lasts for a month or two, but you're stuck with car payments for years and years. Can we ever be satisfied with our possessions, health, families, and environments, or will we always be addicted to our neurochemicals?

The answer for you will depend on whether you can detach yourself from the significance of material goods, peer pressure, and social expectations. If you can focus your attention on things that matter and are important, you will successfully define what enough is for you.

Enough is the opposite of excess. According to Dictionary.com, excess means " An extreme or excessive amount or degree, superabundance. Going beyond what is regarded as customary or proper." Depending on where we grew up, what family we're raised in, and what values we hold will define what extreme or customary is. I would think that owning 35 guns is excessive and improper, but my husband, who hunts and loves guns, thinks that this is an acceptable amount.

Knowing what is enough and what is extreme needs to be put into personal context by asking yourself what is important to you. When you're young, and have the whole world in front of you, you may work 100 hours a week, live in your parents' basement, and eat ramen every night so you can pay off your student loans and save for an apartment deposit. That may not be extreme when you have an end goal. But what about a 50-year-old that's still single, working 100 hours a week, living in their parents' basement, and eating ramen every night so they can pay off their debt? Does the context change here? Is it acceptable for this 50-year-old's behavior compared to a 20-year-old's with the same behavior? Maybe. Maybe the

50-year-old just went through a nasty divorce or a health crisis that created a huge debt and loss of finances in their life. Is this any different from the 20-year-old? Maybe. It's all about the end goal and what's important to you, the context of the situation, so to speak.

Freedom comes at a price. Maybe when we're young, we bust our butts, do what's necessary to climb the corporate ladder, and bury ourselves in the expectations of others. But at some point, we mature and gain some level of success. And we evaluate our life and what we've accomplished and ask ourselves if we want to continue on this same track or if we want to get off the ride.

Most of us will hit this wall in our forties. During this decade, we've started a family, moved up the corporate ladder, and achieved some level of success. Or not. Our bodies and minds begin to slow down. We're not as enthusiastic or ambitious. We long to relax and have some alone time. We strive to carve out a little fun time with our families and friends. We start to look inward instead of outward for our sense of worth and identity.

Usually, at this point, we evaluate our life and define what enough is. We tend to free ourselves from the binds of popular society and its expectations. We simply don't care what people think about us, what we have, or what we've accomplished. We start doing what we want, when we want, and with who we want. We start to feel freedom. We start to take up hobbies that we once enjoyed when we were younger before we had a family and a stressful career. We focus on healthier eating because it makes us feel better and allows us to survive our long days at the office and at home. We take more vacations to exotic places that can create experiences for our families. In essence, we start living for ourselves and not for others.

This is when enough is enough. We take pride in what we've done so far in our lives. How we've contributed to the world with our talents and skills. We have a sense of clarity on where we fit in society and where we don't. We teach the next generation about all the successes and failures that we've gone through so that they may leap ahead of us on their life's journey.

We focus on things that matter to us and say no to the ones that don't. We live from within rather than live from the outer world. We value relationships and experiences over material goods and status. We mature and create instead of competing. We take our time and smell the roses. We write. We dance. We sing. We express ourselves creatively and without regret. We control what we can and let go of what we can't. We strive for bigger causes and take pleasure in smaller ones.

We finally feel we have enough. We finally feel that we are enough, and freedom of our spirits prevails.

Chapter 4

Karma

"Realize that everything connects to everything else."–Leonardo Da Vinci

---

Karma is also known as the Law of Cause and Effect. What you reap, you sow. What you put out into the world, you get out of the world. What actions you take, results will follow. What you think about consistently influences your perception of your reality.

The Golden Rule: Treat others as you would want to be treated.

This truth is universal no matter what religion you believe in, your country, and what century you live in. What you do matters. It matters to yourself and your family. It also matters to other people. Think of all of the technology that is new nowadays. As I write this, everything we do can be stored in the cloud. During my lifetime, we went from landline phones to wireless smartphones. I remember begging my parents to buy a long phone cord so I could have "private" conversations with my friends in the bathroom. The cord they bought could extend from the kitchen, where the phone was attached to the wall, to the bathroom, where I could have my conversations. This was a big deal to a teenage girl. Boy, have things changed!

Now I can be almost anywhere on Earth and talk to someone wirelessly. It truly is an amazing technology that Martin Cooper and his team at Motorola invented in 1973. It would take them another 30 years to develop the wireless network we have today. And it all started with a thought that led to many actions, trials, and errors, and finally, the results we know today.

Karma means "action" in Sanskrit. Buddhism and Hinduism, which originated in India, believe that our actions today can affect our future. If you save and invest money today and allow that money to grow with compound interest, you will have more money in the future. If you eat healthy today and continue that habit, you can avoid diabetes, high blood pressure, heart disease, and even cancer. If you are friendly and can work with other people, you will always find networking and career opportunities in the future. If you plant the seed today in your garden, in a couple of months, you will have a plethora of fruit and vegetables to eat.

That's Karma at its best. The actions you take today will have some kind of effect on your life in the future. But there's also a dark side to Karma. If you keep up with the Joneses and don't save and invest your money, you won't have any to live on during retirement. If you eat poorly and don't exercise, as you age, you will have to deal with diabetes, high blood pressure, heart disease, and even cancer. One of those four things will likely end your life prematurely. If you're not friendly and giving to other people, you will stay at the same job you hate for the rest of your life and will lack fulfillment and purpose forever. I know, it's pretty harsh, isn't it?

The Law of Cause and Effect is similar to Karma in that it states, "Every effect is caused by a certain action, and every cause has some type of effect." Let's take a deeper look into these two similar truths.

The Law of Cause and Effect is my favorite law of the 7 Laws of the Universe. You have The Law of Perpetual Transmutation of Energy, which states that all energy is in motion and can appear in physical form at some point. Think of water. At a certain temperature, water is either in a gas form, liquid, or ice. It's still water, with two hydrogen molecules attached to an oxygen molecule. It's just in a different form.

Then you have the Law of Relativity, which is basically our perception. It's neither good nor bad; it just is. It's neither hot nor cold unless you compare it to something else.

Then we have the Law of Vibration, which is related to the Law of Attraction, which states that everything moves at a certain frequency, even our thoughts. You will get different results if you can think and act in a different frequency or way.

There's the Law of Polarity which states that everything has an equal and opposite. If there's an up, there must be a down. If there's a left, there must be a right. You get the picture.

The next law is the Law of Rhythm which states that everything goes in cycles. Businesses have busy seasons and slow seasons. The weather has seasons, winter, spring, summer, and fall. If we know what season we're in, we can plan our actions to take advantage of the high times. And then there's the Law of Gender which details the male and female energy of life.

All of these laws work together to form the world we live in. If you know these laws, you can maximize everything in life easily and without much effort. If you don't, you'll be constantly stressed and swimming upstream. My favorite, and the one that I think is most useful, is The Law of Cause and Effect.

You can look at this law as the Law of Control. How do you want to live your life? Do you want to be poor? Do you want to be unhealthy? Do you want to be alone? Do you want to be sad? Do you want to be unhappy? If not, you must take control of your thoughts, your emotions, and your actions.

The easiest way to do this is to start thinking of others. We've talked extensively throughout this book about helping others with your natural talents and skills. From finding your purpose to exploring your options in the world. It all matters. We're all put on this Earth for one purpose: to help one another live our best lives. And to do that, we need to take control of our own lives and start taking actions that will allow us to live our best lives.

When we're at our best, others can benefit. Are you more helpful and patient to others if you're well-rested? Are you more creative and innovative if you are in a good mood? If you're ambitious, will you think out of the box more often and go the extra mile? These are all benefits of using The Law of Cause and Effect productively.

To change our realities, we must realize that our realities can easily be changed. Our realities in Metaphysics, according to physicist Tom Campbell, are made up of decisions of future probabilities. We have a past full of actions and results. We have a present that is full of decisions to be made. And we have a future that is uncertain and full of probable outcomes. Which one is in our control right now, this very minute? The present. So how do we make decisions in the present?

The Present

"The point of power is always in the present moment."– Louise Hay

---

Our present is dictated by our environment that constantly stimulates our five senses, all of which are physical senses: touch, taste, smell, sight, and sound. Our realities are shaped by our awareness and understanding/interpretation of those sense stimuli. I may hear a sound and think a machine at my office is not functioning properly. Another person in my office may not be able to tell the differences in the pitch and speed of the sound frequencies to tell the difference. Why? It's because our senses are constricted by our physical bodies. That's why we can't hear the frequency of a dog whistle, but a dog can. This is why a hawk can be high in the sky and see a small rodent numerous feet below it, running for shelter from the hawk's grip. The hawk has sharp eyesight, allowing it to see small rodents and their movements from the sky. We as humans have physical abilities and physical constraints and live our lives by those abilities and constraints.

Our interpretation and understanding of the physical sense stimuli also create our realities. We may be unaware of our ability to set a faster time in the 800m race until our coach gives us different techniques to help us achieve the new faster time. We may be unaware of a tree falling in our backyard because we physically didn't see or hear it as it happened. It's all about our awareness and understanding of our environment that shapes our physical reality.

The good news about this is that we can change it!

In my book, *The Habit Formula: Life's Success Equation*, the first part of the habit formula is your awareness of your current reality. Being aware of the results you're getting can be changed by taking different actions. If you're aware that you make X amount of money for doing X actions, you can learn how to double that by taking different actions. But if you keep making the same X actions, you'll never make Z amount of money. You'll only make X amount of money because the X actions result in X amount of money. It takes Z actions to make Z amount of money. And the only way to learn how to take Z actions to make Z amount of money is to learn and understand the Z actions from someone who gets the Z results you're looking for. It's finding a mentor and taking similar actions to get similar results.

Our realities are based on evolutionary terms. We are always evolving, learning, and growing as a culture, environment, and civilization. Things will always be expanding and getting better over time. It follows Darwin's Theory of Selection which states, "Because resources are limited in nature, organisms with heritable traits that favor survival and reproduction will tend to leave more offspring than their peers, causing the traits to increase in frequency over generations." In other words, only the strongest traits will survive. Only the strongest genes will survive. Only the strongest cultures will survive. Only the strongest ideas and systems will survive. The others will slowly dissolve away. They will be of no use to the new generations evolving and expanding their awareness of the Universe and how things work. It's like the old VCR and corded telephones. We don't need them anymore. They've been replaced with newer technologies.

Our awareness of where we stand in our surroundings creates our realities. After we wake up and look around at our results, can we make the necessary changes to create a new reality and results?

To get into shape, we need to physically measure our bodies. Our weight. The diameter of our limbs and core. We can visit our doctor and get bloodwork done to measure different levels of vitamins and minerals and how well our body works and breaks down the food we eat. This is the rational part of our mind. Once we are aware of our physical results, we can then learn how to change them. We can learn what foods work with our body chemistry to work optimally. We can learn what exercise regime will result in the shape of the body we desire. Then, and only then, can we form an action plan to get us the results we want. Once the plan is formulated, then the only thing we need to do is to make the decision every single day to follow the plan. Of course, that's easier said than done.

To get the results we want, we need to conjure up our inner discipline and willpower. We need to make a conscious effort to exercise and eat every meal according to the plan. We must take the necessary actions to get the results we've planned for. Unfortunately, the plan won't work itself or get the results wanted without us physically and emotionally putting the plan into motion. At first, this is difficult because we must consciously think about the results we want with every meal. Our actions are not habits yet.

According to a 2009 study published in the European Journal of Social Psychology, it takes 18 to 254 days for a person to form a new habit. The study also concluded that, on average, it takes 66 days for a new behavior to become automatic.

We form habitual actions and routines, so our minds don't have to waste critical glucose energy making decisions every second of every day. We all have morning routines where we do the same thing every day. We drive to work the same way because we've figured out the easiest and fastest way to get there. We do our makeup and fix our hair the same way. We cook the same types of meals.

These daily routines and habits help to free the mind from doing other things. To take in new stimuli. To grow and learn different ideas and methods. But it takes effort to make them habits and routines. It takes energy. And it takes willpower and discipline to make the necessary changes to get the results we want and keep making those changes until those actions become routine for us. That's what karma is all about. What we give, we receive.

Most people don't get past two weeks, let alone a possible 254 days. They usually fall off and return to their old way of doing things. Because it's familiar. Because it's safe. It's called the comfort zone. But to grow and change the results we want, we must venture out of our comfort zones and create new habits and routines.

This is also the Law of Cause and Effect. An effect is caused by a certain effort, and a cause gives a certain result. Because we live in a physical universe, we need to take our physical environment and mold it how we want to get the physical results we desire. That's how it works. We can't just think of getting into shape without creating the physical plan of action needed to get there. Of course, positive thoughts can help shape our emotions and actions. But it takes physical actions, moving something and eating something healthy, for the physical results to manifest. Most of us know what to do to be healthy and live a long life, but we don't do it. Why?

Most of the time, it has to do with our comfort zone. We know it will be tough. We know that we will have to eat a lot of things we're not used to or even like to eat. We know we're going to be sore and not be able to move easily for days. We know we will have to be consistent with our exercise and eating. We know that we can get the results we want, but we want the results right now without doing any of the hard work.

Unfortunately, we live in a "magic pill" nation right now. No one wants to put in the effort to correct what's wrong in their lives. They'd rather take a magic pill to solve it for them. They'd rather buy something, so they don't have to put the work in to get the results. But to get the results you're after, you need to put in the hard work that goes along with it.

To make more money, we must first create more value in the marketplace. We need more customers. We need bigger transactions. We need to put in more hours of productivity or less when we become more efficient at getting the desired results. These results take energy, creative thoughts, learned and improved communication skills, and discipline. We must work on these actions every single day so that we can get better at our work and improve our results. We must be positive and helpful and give our talents and abilities to the people and companies needing them. At that point, more money will flow to you. But you must be the cause of the money flow, and the effect will be the money flow.

We must also create good money habits if we want money to hang around in our lives. To be good to us and to be plentiful. In *Happy Money* by Ken Honda, Ken writes, "Start changing your relationship with money by seeing it as your friend." Are you good with money? Do you treat it with respect? Do you use it to help others? Do you invest it so it can multiply, or do you hold onto it and keep it all to yourself? Remember Ebeneezer Scrooge? He was a successful businessman, but the only thing he did was obsess about money. He paid his employees poorly. He was mean to people. Then he had his dream where the ghosts showed him how he could live his life and use his money to help others and build friendships.

That's karma. Anyone can become good with money. Good at being healthy. Good in relationships. Good in their career. But we must learn *how* to be good at those things from people that *are* successful at those things. We must first start changing our relationship with ourselves. We must start with our self-image. We must change our beliefs and attitude toward ourselves and our role in the world. We must have an almost naive belief that anything is possible if we can't fail.

One of my mentors, Peggy McColl, always says, "My success is guaranteed." It's only guaranteed if I don't stop. If I don't quit. If I keep growing, learning, and dreaming. But to get the results we want, we must believe that it's possible. Then we can form the habits and routines that create the results we're after. We can meet the people we want to meet. We can accomplish the goals we want to accomplish. It starts in our minds first. Then it becomes ingrained in our hearts, and only then can it manifest itself in our physical world.

Subjective vs Objective Thinking

"Each person does see the world in a different way. There is not a single, unifying, objective truth. We're all limited by our perspective."-Siri Hustvedt

We must first decipher the difference between subjective and objective thinking to create our realities. Subjective thinking is based on an individual's beliefs and may or may not reflect the beliefs shared by others. Subjective thinking may dismiss facts to align with one's own personal opinions. Subjective thinking is based on an individual's beliefs and may or may not reflect the beliefs shared by others. Objective thinking, on the other hand, deals with facts rather than personal opinions. Facts that the majority of people believe are true or not.

We truly need both to make decisions every day. The best way to achieve the results we want is to start with objective thinking. Find out the facts of the situation. If you want to successfully multiply your money, you need to decide the path you will follow. This involves doing some fact-finding. Do you start or buy an existing company? Do you start investing in real estate? Do you trade stocks? There are only a few paths that you can follow. Then you must find out how long it takes to get involved in those journeys? How much money do you need to have to start investing? Who else needs to be involved to start making money? Banks? Employees? Tenants? Customers? Where are these people? Do they want what you have? What's the market like? What's the pricing for these items? Do I need to create or buy items myself, or is it a service I want to sell? Objective facts must be found before you can start creating the steps needed to follow to end up with the desired results.

After all the facts are uncovered, it's time for your subjective thinking to take over. How do you feel about these different paths? Are you willing to do what it takes to follow a certain path? Does it sound fun to you? Do your skills align with those necessary to move you closer to your wanted results? Do you have any experience one way or another? Do you have people close to you that have gone down one path or another? It's your subjective thinking that will ultimately drive you to your results.

We may think logically (objective thinking) but make decisions emotionally (subjective thinking). We know how to get into shape, but it's too difficult to go to the gym right now, so I'd rather curl up on the couch and watch some Netflix. We can learn all the facts we want, but our emotions about those facts and how far out of our comfort zone it throws us drive our decisions about our actions.

Most people lead average lives because they allow their subjective thinking to dominate their lives. They form their opinions about the world without finding out the facts about a certain issue.

"I could never do that."

"That's for those other people."

"I'm not that type of person."

"We're just not that way."

"That sounds too complicated; I'm okay where I'm at."

"Money isn't everything."

" Money won't make you happy."

"All they do is work out."

"Those other people are just greedy."

"All they do is rip off people."

"Men are only after sex."

"Women are only after money."

Blah, blah, blah.

They form their opinions about what other people are doing and what results they get without first finding out the facts. These opinions don't take into consideration the possibilities of success. Anyone can do anything they want. Even if you live in a Communist country. No one can control your mind and your thoughts except you. There may be obstacles in your way, but nothing is insurmountable.

Everyone *says* they want change, but no one wants to take *action* to change their circumstances. So most people take no action or take the least amount of action necessary to get by, and they never live to their potential. It takes hard work, perseverance, determination, and creative thinking to take your life to the next level. The question you must ask yourself is, "Do you really want it?" If you do, the only way to get there is to be the cause of the effect. To put into motion a series of actions that form a certain pattern of routine that gives you a certain result.

Follow anyone that has success, and you will find the habits and routines that person claimed for themselves on a daily basis. They may not feel like getting up to go practice their fundamentals. But professional athletes are obligated to their team, coach, families, and fans to get up, get dressed, and head to their training facilities. They know that if they put in their hard work during the off-season, they will be ready to do what it takes to be their best during the real season.

Marcus Luttrell said, "You play like you practice and practice how you play." Professional athletes know this. College athletes know this. But this can apply to any situation. If you want to be healthy, you will push your body every single day. You will also fuel your body in a way to maximize its energy and performance. No matter what. No matter how you feel today. No matter what the outside world is doing. No matter what your spouse says or the kids say. No matter what. You give yourself a command, and you follow it. That's called discipline.

Average vs Successful

"Don't settle for average. You were made for greatness."– Victoria Osteen

---

Do you want to be average all your life? Or do you want to excel and push the boundaries of what you think you can do? You can find out all the facts you want about moving up the corporate ladder in your career, but do you have the determination to get there? Are you willing to do whatever it takes to do it?

According to World Data, the average American income for 2020 was just over $69,000. That's gross income. So after paying Uncle Sam, you'd be left with around $50,000 to pay your bills, save money, and invest. That's only $4100 a month. Does this sound like enough money to fuel your dreams? What about giving you the freedom to travel, buy a new car, or save for your kid's college education? Probably not.

Is this your dream? To put in the least amount of effort necessary to be average? What if you put in no effort and live below average? That sounds like fun, huh? People settle for average results because they don't believe they can get different ones. Average people think average thoughts, take average actions and get average results. Average karma.

In *The Secret of Getting Rich,* Wallace Wattles said, "The very best thing you can do for the whole world is to make the most of yourself." If you're average, can you help your community? Do you have enough resources to take care of the handicapped, sick, and debilitated? Can you give your kids a great home to grow up in? Do you have the mental strength to get through hard times? Or do you play the victim and wait for others to come and rescue you?

Do you take control of your mind and body and direct them to perform in a way to give you superior results? Or do you relax and act lethargic because you don't want to strive for anything? Do you worry about what you can't control, or do you control only what you can?

Average people usually think of themselves. They believe that successful people are greedy, mean, and selfish. They don't realize that successful people think of other people continuously; that's why they're successful. They want to help people improve their lives with their products and services. When customers value the business owner's solutions to their problems more than their money, customers part with their money so they can solve their problems. It's a very simple arrangement.

Average people don't contribute much to society. They don't give money and time to charity. They don't think creatively and help people solve their problems. They don't take risks with their money or ideas because they simply don't have any. Average people don't realize that they get paid for the value they bring to the marketplace. If they have important skills and are difficult to replace because of all the value they bring to their company, they can write their own ticket to whatever level of success they want. Average people only do enough to grab their paycheck on Friday, hit the bar or mall, spend all they have, and show up dreading Monday morning when they have to start all over.

Successful people continuously improve themselves. Their health. Their ideas. Their beliefs. Their actions. They open their minds to new ideas and opportunities that come their way. They trust in the process of mentorship. They trust in the process of trial and error. They also trust in themselves and build confidence over time that whatever they want in life, they can go get it. They work hard and expect successful outcomes from their hard work. Average people don't.

The Power of Control

"There are two things a person should never be angry at, what they can help, and what they cannot."-Plato

---

No one can control the outside world; we can only control how we respond to it. Stress comes from the meaning we give to the problem. Worry, anxiety, and fear all come from the unknown. What's the single force that controls the quality of our lives? Tony Robbins said, "It's the power of choice." We can't control the events around us, but we can focus on what they mean. What they mean to us and how it affects our lives.

Our power of choice also comes from the standards that we set. If we don't care how we look, our appearance will reflect that. We won't dress nicely. We won't wear makeup or take care of our hair and skin. We will eat junk food and be overweight. If we decide we don't care, the standards we set for ourselves will also be set pretty low. The inner standards will be reflected as our outer reality. Karma.

Our standards start with all of the decisions we're in control of. We can't play the victim to those decisions because they are our own. We can't blame others for the thoughts and actions we take ourselves. If we hurt someone else, another person didn't control our actions, we did, and there are consequences for our actions. Good and bad. Think of how your life is better because of a decision you've made in the past? How is your life worse because of a decision you've made in the past? Good or bad, we must take responsibility for all of them, and if we don't like the results we're getting, then we need to take different actions.

In his seminars, Tony Robbins says we don't need perfection; we need progress. We need something to strive for. We need some type of goal to force us into action. To make different decisions. To grow and get better. We'll never be done striving for improvement. But we can be satisfied with our daily progress as long as it's carrying us closer to improvement.

Zeno, the founder of Stoicism, said, "Well-being is realized by small steps, but is truly no small thing." Dictionary.com defines well-being as "The state of being comfortable, healthy, or happy." We can't stay comfortable if we want to change something in our life. We can't be healthy if we don't eat the right foods and exercise. We can certainly not be happy if we're not trying to become better people. To learn new things. To raise our standards. To grow as a person and a member in our community.

This doesn't mean we must sacrifice time with our family to pursue our careers. This doesn't mean we sacrifice our health by practicing motorcycle stunts hoping for a million views on YouTube. This also doesn't mean we need to spend all of our money on worthless crap to impress people we don't know or care about. What well-being means is a balance between progress and complacency. We can't be critical of others because *they* are progressing toward *their* goals, and *we* don't progress toward *our* own. We can't feel satisfied with our choices when our results aren't giving us what we want. And we certainly can't contribute to our communities when we have nothing to give.

Peter Sage, a global entrepreneur and business coach, has four areas of identity.

1. To me

2. By me

3. Through me

4. As me

To me people live their lives playing the victim. Everything terrible in their lives was caused by someone or something else, and it always happens to them. They never take the actions necessary to find the progress that they want.

By me people are true Law of Cause and Effect people. These people take actions that cause effects that change their environments and results around them. They do whatever it takes to get the results they are after. But most of the time, they fight against the system. They spend a lot of their resources willing the Universe to bow down to their desires.

Through me people tend to raise their emotions, thus, raising their vibration projected into the Universe. They feel joy, gratitude, love, and fulfillment. Because they seem to have their lives together, they find themselves in situations that can benefit them. More opportunities come their way because they're open to the possibilities and transmit that openness. Their businesses are successful because their customers are always taken care of. They have many relationships because people feel that they're cared for. And they live long, happy lives because they contribute and grow throughout their seasons.

Through me people are also called *lucky* because they tend to be in the right place at the right time. They do this because they project helpfulness and confidence. There's no desperation in their voice. People love talking to them because they drive the conversation toward the other person, not themselves. They allow forces to flow through them to other people and go with the flow downstream instead of battling life upstream. I know, it's crazy.

As me people are very spiritual and tend to live on the metaphysical plane. They aren't concerned with their physical possessions. They are always increasing their vibration and frequency to match that of God or the universe. This is definitely a level of living worth striving for, but I'm not sure it's a realistic modern approach to the world we live in today.

Karma is classically displayed through the actions of *by me* people and allowed to happen to *through me* people. The question is, what type of person do you want to become? Do you want to make things happen, or do you want things to happen to you? Can you control your thoughts and open your mind to new ideas and actions, or will you turn away from other people and keep to yourself. It's all about the daily decisions that we make in our lives. Decisions that are controlled *by us* and can be *for us* if we allow them to be.

Greg McKeown, in his book *Essentialism*, says it this way, "No one can take away your right to choose. You can't even give it away if you want. You can only forget that you have the power to decide." You can decide how you want to live. You can decide if you want to play the victim (to me) or take control of your life (by me and through me.) It's all up to you. Decide. Control your choices. No one's stopping you except you. Decide what you want. Decide to change. Who cares what other people do? Who cares what other people say? They don't pay your bills. They're not living your life. Tune out other people and decide what you want your life to look like. If you don't like your present condition, then change it. Remember that changing one small thing is no small change. One change can result in many changes in different areas of your life. Decide to change one thing today. You won't regret making the decision and acting on it today. Don't wait. Change!

Today

"Carpe diem- seize the day." -Horace

We all need things to look forward to. The power of hope. We need to create margin in every area of life. Extra money. Extra relationships. Extra time. We need to ensure that we're not living our lives according to someone else's agenda. We must make sure that we're living the way we want to live each day. Spending time with our family and friends. Having some fun. Eating some great food. Drinking our favorite beer. Taking a walk and enjoying where we live. Calling a friend and giggling like a couple of teenagers.

We can't allow the obligations we've set up for ourselves to take the place of the simple pleasures in our lives. A smile. Holding hands with our lover. Coloring with our child. When exactly can we plan these things in our lives? There's truly no planned time for these things. We must do them when the urges arise. We must take the time and act now, or the time for our obligations will drown out our memory-creating time.

We must say no. We must take responsibility for the resources we have. Our time. Our energy. Our money. Who will control our resources if we don't control them? That's what today is for. That's what right now is for. Think of something you want to do, maybe a hobby you haven't done yet. What about your favorite food or recipe? What about a friend you haven't talked to or seen in a while. Don't hesitate. Right now, go do that thing or talk to that person that's been on the back burner for too long. Grab the bull by its horns and ride them! Carpe diem- seize the day, right? Make today one of the best days you've had in a long time. Do the thing and see that person you want to see. No excuses. No procrastination. No second-guessing. Be intentional!

If you want to enjoy your life, enjoy the present time. Enjoy where you're at right now, doing what you're doing right now, with the person or persons you're doing it with. Do it right now! Don't wait because you and I both know that there is always something else you could be doing. There's always some other obligation that could be taking up your resources. But does that obligation need to be done right now? Or could you spare some time and energy to have some fun and smell the roses a little? Take a break and spend some time doing something fun. Something creative. Something that makes you feel alive.

The Law of Rhythm

"We all share the same cosmic rhythm. For all natural laws are like the rhythm of the strings of the harp." – Ernesto Cardenal

---

The Law of Rhythm states that all things move in rhythm or cycles. Seasons, tidal waves, moon phases, and even our bodies move through different cycles. Think of economic cycles. We have years when the country and the stock market are in bull phases. Supply and demand are equal, and the prices of goods and services remain in check with inflation. Companies sell their goods successfully and make profits rewarding their shareholders with their own profits in their investment portfolios.

But then there are years when the demand for products and services far exceeds the supply, and inflationary pricing goes through the roof. Companies don't make as many profits, thus experiencing downturns in their stock pricing, and their clients' portfolios take a hit. These are called bear markets.

The good thing about cycles and the Law of Rhythm is that all cycles change. If they're down, they will start to turn back up. If they're up, then they start to round the top and decline. It's a huge wave. Up and down. Down and up. Always changing. Always moving. Every business has busy seasons and slow seasons. Every relationship has a new excitement and a boring, nearing-to-end phase. Up and down. Good and bad. Fast and slow.

The Law of Cause and Effect and karma tie directly into the Law of Rhythm if you can catch it. What do you do when your business is in a slow phase? To change the bottom line, you need to take some kind of action to start changing things. You make more calls. You follow up with your customers more often. You trim team members that aren't pulling their weight. You track spending and improvement expenditures more carefully. You tighten your spending habits and use that money to market your business more. You take every action necessary to change the down phase of your business into a growing up phase. You take action. You cause an effect. You change. You grow. That's using the Law of Rhythm to your advantage. You're aware of your company numbers and what phase you're in. You know it won't last forever. But you know that you can speed up the growth trajectory if you take certain actions, as previously mentioned, and start to stir things up.

What about the general economic cycles? People generally freak out when the word *recession* is mentioned. Obviously, we can either think *dread* or we can think of opportunity. The 2020 Covid pandemic really opened people's eyes to how they were spending their money. I took the opportunity to get my financial house in order, personally and professionally. I paid off almost all my debt over the course of 18 months, including my house and car. I socked away 50% of my income to invest in real estate, digital real estate domains, oil, gold, and the stock market. As the high inflation rates marked 2023 as I write this book, I'm taking all the extra capital I have and sinking it into the stock market S & P 500 Index Funds. The market currently is down over 25%. This means that everything is on sale right now! Because the stock market is backed by real physical companies producing goods and services, the likelihood that the market will bounce back and achieve even higher returns is a no-brainer.

Warren Buffet, one of the most successful investors of all time, said, "Be greedy when people are fearful, and fearful when people are greedy." When the herd goes one way, does that mean you have to follow it? When people are freaking out that their portfolios are down 30%, is this a reason to panic, or is it an opportunity to invest more?

In 2022, the main cryptocurrencies that had been all the rage for the past few years have really taken a hit. I didn't take any positions in crypto because I didn't understand it. It's all made up. It was created to decentralize the banking system so people could buy goods using cryptocurrencies without the government and banking industry knowing what was happening. The problem is that there's no regulation in it. It's just a computer program that someone made up that's housed on thousands of computers around the world (blockchain). No one is using it as a payment method which is what it was intended to be. Okay, but there's no real tangible value in any of it. The only way my crypto goes up is if someone else buys a share for a higher price than what I bought it for. Now if people were actually buying goods using crypto, it would then build extrinsic value like paper money does. But for now, it's a big joke, and the market reflects that.

I am living through yet another market downturn. I'm unsure what that will mean for my dental practice and business. But I know I will be very weary about making any big purchases over the next couple of years unless it will pay me money in the near future. I know I'm in a much better financial position today in 2023 than in 2019 due to having little to no debt. All of the money I spend paying off debt is now being used to buy assets. Stocks. Real estate. Digital real estate domains. Gold and silver. Oil. Forex bots. And when the markets are down, I have the money to buy. When the markets go back up, I still buy, but at a slower rate, knowing that if I can store some cash on the side, I can wait for the next downturn and buy even more assets that are on sale.

When they say, "Cash is trash," it depends on what they are referring to. If you're talking about investments, cash really is king. If you have extra cash sitting on the sideline, you can jump on opportunities that unfold in the marketplace. Cash itself isn't worth much, but you can buy assets with it that would generally be out of your reach. That's the Law of Rhythm at its best. Being prepared. Being aware of what part of the cycle you're in today and what you must do to prepare for the change in the cycle in the future. Being intentional with your money and your future. Do you need cash? Do you need patience? Do you need to trim the budget? Do you need to change products or services? Do you need to change people or jobs? It's all about being aware of the present moment and taking advantage of the cycles as they change.

You can use the Law of Rhythm in your personal life too. Let's say you've been in a relationship for a while, and things are beginning to turn dull and mundane. What do you do? Maybe it's time for an exciting vacation? Maybe you need time with your mate to rekindle your relationship and ensure you're on the same wavelength. Your relationship needs attention, too, just like a living plant needs water and food. Your relationship needs attention and focus. It needs to be nurtured. Maybe you need to hire a babysitter and have a fun date night. Maybe you need to surprise your lover with their favorite meal. Maybe you plan a crazy night of hot sex. Whatever brings awareness and intentionality to your relationship is the course of action you should take.

Most divorces happen over the course of many months and even years. No one just decides they want out of their marriage. Their marriage dies a slow death because no one is paying attention to their relationship. No one works on bringing the excitement and fun back into it, and it slowly withers and dies. That's why people cheat. It's not to intentionally hurt their significant other. It's because they're not getting the same dopamine and serotonin rush they used to have when their relationship was fresh and new. So they look for their hormone rush with someone else. Be intentional with your relationship and pay close attention to it. And you'll continue feeling those good hormones that will help to keep your relationship fresh and new.

What about your health? If your clothes are feeling tight, you know it's time to change your eating and exercising habits. It's time to get intentional with your health. It takes time to gain weight and get pudgy. It will take time to undo the damage. But that's okay. Everyone gets distracted by life circumstances. Maybe the holidays messed you up. Maybe you're stressed at work and haven't been eating at your normal time. It doesn't really matter. You know that you're in a down cycle of your health, and now you must change the actions that you're taking so that you can once again feel good. It's time to be intentional!

Living intentionally is about having the knowledge of the cycles of life as well as your mindset and perception about it. It takes energy to be aware of where you are in your cycles, whether professionally or personally. If you are aware of your position, you can easily take the measures necessary to change it. But it will take time, money, and energy to start changing your circumstances. And that's okay. It takes time for things to change, good or bad. So being aware of the cycles and what steps you need to take to change them in the right direction will make a difference in your life. You can either live your life going with the flow of the cycles, or against it.

Chapter 5

Simplicity

"The secret of happiness, you see, is not found in seeking more, but in developing the capacity to enjoy less."–Socrates

---

During the Covid pandemic, I did a lot of soul-searching and started to analyze why I was doing the things I was doing. Pretty deep stuff, huh? One thing that I realized was that things seemed to get a lot simpler. We weren't going out as much, and it seemed like my stress level was going down. My patient load at the practice wasn't as high, so I had more time to concentrate on running the business instead of allowing the business to run me. When it was all said and done, my life became simpler.

This all seems weird as I'm writing it, but in essence, that's what happened. And I loved it! I loved not rushing around every day trying to get in all the things on my *To Do* list. I loved not being obligated to travel to my family or in-laws. I loved that my finances were simpler and controlled with my budget.

I simply developed the strength to say, "No!" And it felt liberating. I've since said no to a lot of other things in my life. I rarely watch Netflix, but I was thumbing through the documentaries and stumbled upon one called, *The Minimalists*. In summary, it was about a couple of young guys who were in the middle of the corporate rat race and decided to get out of it by simplifying their lives and possessions.

By owning fewer possessions, they spent less money, which meant they didn't need to work eighty-hour weeks. They didn't need to organize or clean their clutter because they didn't have any. They decided to simplify their lives and start their journey of minimalism. This decision spilled out from their possessions to their time, energy, and finances.

After watching the documentary, I decided that I would take on their 30-day challenge of getting rid of stuff for 30 days. I then stumbled on two more YouTube stars, Joshua Becker and Gabe Bult, who also adopted the minimalist lifestyle. Being in my 40s with a family, a career, and responsibilities, I really identified with Joshua but also got a lot of good information and tips from Gabe.

Joshua suggested going through a room, grabbing a box or bag, and randomly getting rid of anything that didn't bring value, joy, or purpose to my life. Three weekends and 63 bags and boxes later, my house was clutter free and looked neat and organized. I couldn't believe how much extra stuff I had accumulated over the past decade that we had lived in that house.

I remember when we had moved into the house, I had decluttered a lot of stuff before the move, so I didn't have to move as much stuff. During this project, I realized that most of the stuff I got rid of, donated, or sold was stuff that I didn't even buy. It was stuff gifted to me by friends or family members at Christmas or my birthday.

My husband was not on board at first, thinking that my donating piles were a waste of good money. But as the house started to look neat and clean, I didn't ask him as much for help. He got on board quickly. After we had decluttered his hunting room and got rid of eight boxes and bags, he soon saw the benefits of living with intention and not cluttering it up with stuff.

I want to live a simple life. I want to do what I want, when I want, and with who I want. I don't want to feel obligated to go somewhere. I don't want to feel stressed because the house is a wreck. I've worked hard all day, and now I have to clean up our crap and put it away? No, thank you.

Over the past few months, I've also decided to declutter my office. I've always kept my office neat and organized. I use the same tools and do things the same way to get a predictable result. This allows me to do things quickly and efficiently because, let's face it, no one likes to go to the dentist. So I try my best to get things done quickly so the patient can get out of my chair without stressing out.

One of the big hassles every small business owner has in their life is paper. Keeping receipts can become pretty daunting. It's been easier during this digital age to use a scanner to scan all of the receipts into my computer and organize them into categories in case we're ever audited. But this still takes time. I am always relieved and grateful on scanning day because I can put all those receipts in the shredder and have a nice clean desk!

But it didn't stop there. I had a whole closet full of dental and marketing books, CDs, and DVDs that I wasn't using anymore. So again, it took me a couple of weeks, but I went through everything. I got rid of 70% of my stuff that was just sitting in my closet, not bringing any value to my life or my business.

It felt great! It felt liberating! It felt calming. That's what minimalism or simplifying has done for me. It has allowed me to live more intentionally. I don't randomly make an impulse purchase at the store, saving me money that I am using to pay off my house. During my decluttering, I asked myself, "Do you need this?" My husband was a big, just-in-case kinda guy, but I would ask him if he had used that item over the past month or even year. Once he saw the value in only having the stuff he used, he became calmer too.

Becoming a minimalist isn't a cult. It doesn't mean that our rooms are bare or we don't spend money on anything. Minimalism, for us, simplifies our lives. Cleaning out the clutter frees our time, energy, and money resources. If we don't have as much stuff, we have more money and time that we're not using on organizing to spend in other ways.

We had a lot of electronics and musical instruments that I decided to sell. I got $1219 for all of it when it was all said and done! There were gaming systems that we never used anymore and old guitars and speakers that no one was using. We used that money to start renovating our master bathroom. So not only was this stuff just sitting there and cluttering up our third bedroom but it wasn't being used. Why not give it to someone that could use it?

My son was pretty good throughout the whole decluttering process. He helped me take stuff out of drawers, clean out his room, and bring the stuff to donate. At times, he couldn't believe how much stuff we had packed in the back of my car. I told him to make sure when he got older to not waste his money on stuff that didn't bring him value or happiness. If he didn't waste his money, he wouldn't have to work as hard to make it and could spend it on stuff he really wanted.

I mean, how many spatulas does one person need? How many clothes do you need? How many video games do you need? How many extra blankets and pillows do you need, just in case?

I found that my decluttering activity greatly made me question my wants versus my needs. I may have wanted these things in the past, but I didn't need them over time. I didn't use them or remember having many of them. Why were they still in my house if I didn't remember I had them? Why were they still in my office in a closet?

Minimalism can also be called simplicity. Simplicity leads to purpose, and simplicity can spill out into other areas of our lives. We've talked about money and intentionality all throughout this book. Simplicity can help in both areas. Simplicity can allow us to get rid of social pressures and focus our resources on what truly makes us happy.

This includes our relationships with others and our relationship with our stuff. How often have we tripped over something that had been in our way for the past week, month, or even year? What was it doing there? Obviously, it needed to be put away and out of the walking area. Or maybe it was there because we didn't have use for it and it didn't require a home. So why not get rid of it?

Why do we own so much stuff and are best friends with our Amazon delivery guy or gal? Why do we yearn for the latest electronics or gadgets that come on the market? Why do we care so much about what others think of us if we don't get that upgraded trinket? It's okay to live a more simple and more meaningful life. It's okay to live with intention and purpose and have money in the bank for a rainy day. It's okay to save and invest our money so that we don't have to work as hard the older we get. It's not only okay to live this kind of life, but it's really cool too!

How many debt-free people do you know? How many people do you know have a couple of million dollars in investments? How many people don't have to work 40 hours a week? How many people can take a walk in the middle of the afternoon or sit and read under a shady tree enjoying the sunshine on a Tuesday? Not many.

Why does simplicity scare people? Why do we make everything so complicated? Simplicity doesn't mean inferiority. Life doesn't have to be complicated. Complicated situations take more resources to unravel. Complicated people never get ahead because they're so wrapped up in their minor things that they never spend their resources on major things. Stop complicating things!

Live with intention. Take back control of your life and resources. Wouldn't it be nice to not have monthly payments eating away at your hard-earned income? Wouldn't it be nice to hang out with your kids on the weekend and not have anything on your calendar that you were *obligated* to do? Wouldn't it be nice to have the time to work out or practice the hobby you used to love before you worked or had a family?

It *can* be done. To live this way, something has to give; an easy way to do this is to simplify. An easy place to start is with your possessions. Start with a closet and donate or sell clothes you haven't worn in a year, two, or three. Get rid of the things stuffed in the corners, boxes, and shelves you never use but possess, *just in case*. Look at your desk and wipe the surface clean. Empty out drawers of all the broken electronics and cords that are outdated and useless.

Once your house is simplified and clean and tidy, look in your calendar and start simplifying the obligations you signed up for. Prioritize who gets part of your most precious resource, time. Decide which activities you want to participate in and which ones you don't. This includes your children's activities too. Simplify their lives. If they've never had a home-cooked meal because you're running them all night to sporting activities, something is wrong here. One or two activities is plenty. Everyone, including your children, needs some downtime to relax and regroup. There's nothing wrong with coming home after a long day at school, hanging out, playing games, or watching TV.

Start unsubscribing to all of the advertisements that tempt you daily in your email account about sales for things you really don't need. All that these advertisements do is help you part with your money. If you don't know that Nordstrom's is having a sale on boots that you already have too many of, then you won't be tempted to buy another pair that will sit in the closet, taking up space with the rest.

If we're not spending all of our money on things we don't need to impress our Instagram followers, then we don't have to work as hard to make all of that money. Then we have more time and energy to do things in our life that make us happy. That fulfills us. That makes a difference to us and those around us.

If we had more time, energy, and money, what would we do with it? Would we spend more time with our friends and loved ones? Sure. Would we start playing the piano again because we had the time and energy to practice? Sure. Would we sit down without electronics and have a wonderful home-cooked meal with our family? Sure. Could we go on a paid-for vacation to a place we've never been? Sure.

The possibilities are endless when we simplify our lives and live them with intention. As humans, we want to expand. We want to improve. We want more. It's an innate intuition that all of us have. But in today's society, we tend to fill the void we have for more with material possessions, as we discussed earlier in the book. We want it all, and we want it now. We never slow down and enjoy the present moments. We are always pushing and shoving and spending our precious resources on more, more, more. Then we end up exhausted, frustrated, and broke, and we wonder why.

I think that's why we end up having our mid-life crisis in our 40s. Mine came at 44. My body was hurting. I was completely bored and frustrated at work and wondered what I was missing. I finally figured out that I was missing my purpose. Somehow, as I was pushing and shoving to accumulate more and more, I pushed myself off track. Then when I looked around, I didn't recognize who I was or where I was going.

Have you ever had that happen? Some people don't make it to their mid-life crisis time to figure out that they're not living the life they want. They're the lucky ones. Some people never figure out that they have control over their actions and resources until it's too late and they die living their life for others.

For me, I decided to take control of my life. I cut back on the hours I spent in my dental practice. I only worked three days a week. I started a writing hobby that I always enjoyed but lacked the time and mental energy to pursue. I started to work out and control my diet. I started going out more and even started the Beer Divas YouTube channel to have more fun. I cleaned out my house of all the clutter. I controlled my finances with my budget and made retirement investing a top priority. I cleared my weekends to spend time with my husband and my child. We did more things together. We had more adventures together. We built more memories. It all came down to one word: simplify.

Have you ever wondered where the time went? You had a huge *To Do* list, and you got lost in all of the activities on the list and looked up at the clock to realize that the day was gone and it was time for dinner. What about money? Did you ever get paid on Friday, check your bank account on Tuesday, and wonder where all of your money went? What about your energy? Have you felt like you were run over by a bus, and it's only Wednesday?

I think we've all been there. We've allowed our resources to be used by circumstances that we've allowed to be out of control. We've piled on too many obligations that waste our time and energy. We've spent too much money on things that we don't need. We've allowed *others* to control us instead of *us* taking control. It's really easy to pile things up and deplete our resources. It's more difficult to simplify and realize that we only have so many resources to go around.

No, we can't do it all! I know this comes as a shock to all of the feminists in the world, but there's only so much time, energy, and money to go around. Why not spend the resources we have doing the major things in our lives? If we have resources left over, we can spend them on other things. But instead, we do things backward. We say yes to things that take away our resources. We say yes to things that take us off course. We say yes to things that don't matter. The question is, why?

Do we feel guilty about not making cupcakes for our kid's class? Maybe. Do we feel guilty that we don't help our coworkers on their projects because they know we can? Maybe. Do we feel a sense of shame that we are driving an old, rusty car when we're driving a client around looking at houses? Maybe. What we don't understand is that nobody cares. Nobody is looking at you. Nobody is judging you. Nobody is paying attention to you. It's all about them. That's the only person they are worried about. It's WIIFT (what's in it for them!)

Maybe women feel this more than men, I don't know, but the "mommy guilt" thing is real. I thank the women's movement for that. I don't get to just work all day. But now, I get to come home, be a super wife and super mom, and do everything for everybody until I collapse for the night and wake up and do it all over again the next day. No thank you, women's movement. I'm permanently off that hamster wheel.

I don't feel guilty or obligated anymore, and you shouldn't either. Why? Because I simply don't care what other people think of me or my actions. If you work all day, don't fill your nighttime with activities and obligations that spend all of your resources and really don't matter in the long run. Look at the big picture and ask yourself what's important. Do you really want to sign up your kid for travel baseball when he's the smallest kid on the team and can't catch a ball if it is attached to his glove? Why spend the money or time on that? Do you really want to spend time organizing all of the stuff in your house every night because it's in the way? Do you want to work an extra side gig because you're in debt from spending too much money on things you don't need? Come on, let's think about this for a second.

Why do we need to buy a new car when the old one works fine and is paid off? Why are we overweight, eat junk, and never exercise? Why do we constantly want more of the things that aren't good for us, don't get us toward our goals, or don't make us happy? For some reason, we allow chaos to control our lives.

But that can change in an instant. For me, I remember watching a PBS special on eating more fat to lose weight. I decided then that I was going to change my diet for good. I learned how to eat better and with fewer carbs. I instantly lost weight. I gave up dairy after finding out I had an allergy to whey protein. I started to feel better. My body didn't hurt anymore. I started to have more energy. This spilled out professionally. I cut back on my hours treating patients. I started writing and creating content. My mind became more clear and energized. I found the minimalists and started simplifying my physical possessions, obligations, and goals. My stress level plummeted. I started having fun. I started creating. I started being a better person, all from making a split-second decision to make a change.

One change led to another. And another. And another. I am four years into my journey, and I am still evolving. I have finally realized that I can make things as simple or as complicated as I want. I choose simple. And it's working. I am in control of my life. I control who I spend my time with. I control how I spend my money. I control where I spend my energy. This control that I'm feeling is true freedom. Freedom to live the way I want. My life is still a work in progress, but these past few years have been wonderful. I don't feel trapped. I don't feel stretched too thin. I feel great in my own skin. I'm proud. I'm thankful. I feel love for others and feel loved by them. I'm truly happy, and if I find something I'm not happy with, I change it.

Maybe that's awareness or awakening. Maybe that's being in my fourth decade. Or maybe it's just the realization that I'm back on track and living up to my potential. Whatever it is, I'm glad I figured it out before it was too late. I love that I can live the rest of my life, no matter how long or short it is, being happy, content, and fulfilled.

How do you want to live *your* life? Being tired? Frustrated? Broke? Worried? Helpless? You know you can change it in a split second. You can get back to the ol' days when life was simpler. Before the internet. Before societal pressure. Before expectations. Leading a simple life isn't unsophisticated or unintelligent. It's quite the opposite. Those that control their resources are some of the most intelligent and sophisticated people in the world. They have chosen to use their resources the way they want. They know what enough is.

Look at Elon Musk. He recently sold all of his houses and rents a tiny home near his SpaceX headquarters. Steve Jobs and Mark Zuckerberg wore the same types of clothes daily to simplify their morning decisions. Jeff Bezos solves complicated problems using a "5 why root cause analysis," which looks at what simple causes result in these problems. Warren Buffett lives in the same house that he bought in 1958. He has a very simple investment strategy: look at companies as a whole and invest in ones that are run well and have the potential for growth. He only owns 65 companies, but they are worth over $873 billion.

Our lives don't have to be complicated to be successful. We don't have to own four closets of clothes. We don't have to drive Lamborghinis or travel by private jets. We don't have to own ten credit cards and max all of them out to look successful.

We can spend our time selfishly with who we want, doing the things we want. We don't owe anyone anything! We can live on a farm, grow our veggies, and write a blog that sustains our monthly expenses. We can work on our computers remotely while we travel the world. We can live in a Suburb with a white picket fence and play cornhole in the backyard if that's how we want to live.

The American dream is alive if we learn to control what we can and let the rest go. The rest doesn't matter. The rest is all showmanship. The rest is what is stopping us from living the way we want. The rest is keeping us in debt, from being healthy, and feeling like a hamster going around the wheel of our lives. We need to control our resources, so they don't control us!

Why do we want to complicate everything? Why can't we focus on the task ahead of us and pour our resources to the best of our ability on that one task? That's how big things happen. Seneca, an ancient Roman stoic philosopher and statesman said, "Every day, acquire something that will fortify you against poverty, against death, indeed against other misfortunes, as well." If we're creating chaos in our lives, we can't prepare ourselves for misfortunate circumstances.

If we spend all of our resources on minor things that don't matter or push our boundaries in the direction we want, we will be bankrupt when we need them the most. So the next question is, "How do I simplify my life?"

Even though this concept of simplification is, in other words, simple, it's not necessarily easy. To simplify means to break things down into their basic forms. If you want to lose weight, what will this entail? We need a certain amount of time to carve out during our day to exercise. We will need a certain amount of money to purchase the necessary supplements, healthy foods, and equipment per se needed to give our body what it needs to succeed. Then we must make mental space where we listen to a trainer or reference a certain cookbook to create meals and exercise routines to get us to our target weight. This mental space also includes our will. One of the mental faculties that need to be dusted off and invigorated through inspirational quotes and encouragement from outside sources to help us start and continue with our goal of losing weight.

Okay, now we have all of the ingredients needed to develop a simple daily plan that will become a routine and eventually a lifelong habit that can ultimately change the course of our life. But we must first focus on acquiring all of the ingredients before starting this new plan.

Then we follow the plan. We don't have to think about it anymore. We don't have to research it or wonder if the plan we've designed is right for us. All we have to do now is follow the plan. That completely simplifies things, doesn't it? You've already done all the research and taken action to create the plan. Now, it's time for action. It's the action that will get the results. First is the desire, then comes the research, then comes the plan, and finally comes the action that leads to the results. Simple, right?

Let's say you want to become debt free. First, you must collect the information to know exactly how much debt you owe. Then you must know how much you're bringing in and how much you're spending (and on what). Then you can create a plan to move your finances around. You can cut out things that aren't necessary, thus creating a surplus of funds that can be put on the debt every paycheck. After you know your budget, you follow it every month. The results will be obvious after a certain amount of time. You will be debt free if you follow your plan. You know what you have to do. All you have to do is follow the plan.

It takes a lot of guts and discipline to follow through on your goals. Bob Proctor, one of the stars of the movie, *The Secret* says, "Discipline is the ability to give yourself a command and then follow it." For some reason, we want to stray from the plan. We give every excuse in the book for why we stray.

"I didn't feel like it."

"This will never work for me."

"If only I _____, then I could do it."

"When _____ happens, then I can do it."

"I deserve to treat myself."

"It's too hard."

"I'm not _____ enough."

Blah, blah, blah. We have become a society of excuses and blame. We blame others for the way our lives pan out. We blame the government. We blame the weather. We blame our parents. We blame our color, our genetics, and our inheritance. It's time to wake up! It's time to blame the only person responsible for your life: you. Grow up. Grow some guts, take the action you already know how to do, and make your life the way you want it.

The average person only lives for 4160 weeks. That's around 80 years. How many weeks have you already spent? I'm 49, which means I only have roughly 1,586 left if I hit 80. Of course, I want to hit 100 or more, but nothing in life is certain except that we will all die. *Memento Mori*- remember death. The old question, "How do you eat an elephant? One bite at a time." What bite will you be taking today, this hour, this minute? Tomorrow may never come; the present time is all that we have. Now is the best time to make a decision about your life, start researching, create a plan, and then execute it.

Nothing we do today is new. Our tribulations. Our relationships. Our life journeys. We are born, live, and then die, just like thousands of generations of humans for the past 200,000 years. We've only lived in civilized, organized societies for around 6,000 years. But somehow, we think that tomorrow will be better. That tomorrow will be different, so we wait for tomorrow, but tomorrow never comes. Only today is here. Only in the present can we make the decision to simplify our lives and focus on the things that really matter to us.

Getting a brand-new phone, car, or jeans may be exciting and give you an adrenaline dump, but that's all it is; it's a dump. It will use your resources and dump them into someone else's pocket instead of your own. Yeah, you may feel cool or in style or important when you squander your resources on frivolous things, but one thing we can't get back is time. And over time, good things can happen as well as bad things. What if our health fails? What if something happens to a loved one? What if we lose our job? What if we don't get 4,000 weeks, we only get 2,000 or 1,500? Can we rest at night knowing that we lived life to our potential or that we just took up space and now it's over? So, who cares?

We can't improve civilization unless we free our obligations. We can't solve our planet and societal problems unless we have the necessary resources. To do this, we must go to the basics. We must focus on what we can control, which is ourselves. We can't control what other people think, feel, or do, but we can control ourselves. You can't control what governments do, what your boss says, or how your spouse feels. All you can do is control you. And when you decide to focus your attention and resources toward the things that matter to you, you'll let go of all the other distractions surrounding you and simplify. You'll simplify your possessions. You'll simplify your obligations. You'll simplify how you perceive life and the situations that occur in it.

By simplifying, you create a surplus of resources that can be used to your discretion. You get to be in charge of how these resources are spent. Isn't that exciting? Isn't it liberating? Don't you feel relieved? No longer do you have to live in a chaotic environment where people are taking your money, spending your time, and ruining your physical and mental health. No longer will you feel as though there's no control and that life is hopeless. You will no longer need to create excuses for what is; instead, you can create a plan for what will be. Wow. That needs to be on a T-shirt.

The future cannot be controlled. The only thing that can be controlled is right here and now. The present time. Only today can you move the needle on your goals. Only today can you decide to take your life in a different direction. Only today matters. Are you up for the challenge?

Don't wait until you're 44 to make the change or take control like I did. Simplify your life and use your resources to live a wonderful 4,000 weeks. Minimize, simplify, and clarify the things that matter in your life. If they don't matter, let them go. What matters to me may not necessarily matter to you, and that's what makes us all special and unique. The surplus of resources allows our society to thrive and advance. What will you do today to help your country, community, and family? What resources do you have that can be spent to improve your life?

Time. Money. Energy. Attention. These are the only resources we have. These are the resources that are precious and must be guarded. These are the resources that need to be simplified.

Chapter 6

Health

"A healthy man wants a thousand things, a sick man only wants one."–Confucius

---

When we're young, we think that we're invincible. We ride our bikes over the rocks. We jump, skip, and wrestle with bigger kids. We drink too much, fall in the bushes, and tear our ACLs. We eat all the Taco Bell we can manage because it's cheap. We drink our Red Bulls and our Monster Drinks. We're up all night and sleep all day. Yes, that is a song by Slaughter in the 1990s. We listen to loud music. We scream. We play our favorite sports and visit the hospital and the surgeon once in a while to put us back together.

When we're young, we don't realize that we're destroying the very thing that will help get us to old age: our body. Yes, I believe we're spiritual beings living in a body and having a human experience. Let's get that out of the way right now. But we still live in these bodies. And think about it, we're only here for a short amount of time, and that time depends on our physical bodies.

In 2023, the average expected lifespan of a male, according to SimplyInsurance.com is 76 years, and for a female, it's 81 years. That's 912 months for men and 972 months for women. That's 47,424 weeks for men and 50,544 weeks for women. That's 331,968 days for men and 353,808 days for women. When you do the math on our lifetimes, it doesn't seem that long. Does it? According to statistics on statista.com, only 573,000 people in the world reached 100 years of age. That's out of 7.7 billion people. That's a .007% chance that you'll reach 100 years of age.

If you smoke, eat processed and fast food, love sugar, drink alcohol, and live a sedentary lifestyle, your chances of reaching 100 are pretty slim to none. If you have cancer, high blood pressure, diabetes, or heart disease, your chances of reaching 100 are also pretty slim to none.

So how do we have fun and be adventurous without doing permanent harm to our bodies?

For the answer, we must turn yet again to my favorite philosophers, the Stoics. And the answer comes from one of their core virtues, moderation. Our bodies are truly miraculous. It can heal itself. It can regulate itself. It can rejuvenate itself. But there's a point when the body can't. There's a breaking point that prevents the body from doing its normal thing, and that point is simply treating the body with excess harm. Excess exercise. Excess stress. Excess sugar. Excess toxins. Excess injury. Excess extremes.

Once we break the body's natural homeostasis and rhythm of function, all havoc will break loose. This comes in the form of cancer. Cancer is simply cells that don't replicate as they should. Cancer cells don't follow suit if your stomach cells replicate in a certain way and at certain times. In any part of the body, these cancerous, non-functioning cells can replicate and spread throughout the body, causing other tissues and organs to replicate and become non-working. When enough of our tissues and organs don't work, we die. It's as simple as that.

When we soak our tissues with sugar and excess toxins like cigarettes, vaping, and alcohol, we stress the liver in charge of absorbing and degrading toxins that enter the body. But there's only so much detoxification the liver can do; if it stops working, *you* will stop working.

And what about the extreme athletes? Not only are they constantly injuring their skeleton and musculature systems, but they're also causing extreme use of their cardiovascular and pulmonary systems. Have you ever known a guy who loves to run, has never been sick in his life but dies at 52 from a heart attack? A lot of these guys have no family history of heart disease, no cholesterol problems, and are in great physical shape. So what happened? It's called extreme usage. Humans aren't meant to push themselves to the extremes physically for decades.

As we age, our DNA can become damaged. Toxins, pesticides, and exposure to X-rays can damage the DNA of our cells, which is responsible for cell repair and duplication. If our cells don't replicate correctly, they also won't work correctly. If your liver cell isn't replicated correctly, how will your liver detoxify and heal your body? It won't. Many times, this can result in cancerous tumors. These tumors happen because DNA replication has gone awry, and the cells don't function as they did in the past. If these cells make up a vital organ such as the brain, lung, kidney, or liver, the chances of survival decrease significantly.

According to National Geographic, our body comprises over 37 trillion cells. That's a lot of cells. Think of all the cells in your body doing their jobs, replicating, and then dying. Studies from Stanford University stated that our bodies recreate themselves every seven to ten years.

So think about that for a minute. We become an entirely new and different person every decade. This makes a lot of sense so far in my own life. As I have aged, I have noticed that my hair is different. It's more wavey than it used to be. I'm getting more gray hair that's curly. I'm storing fat in different parts of my body. I've had to change my diet because I discovered I had a severe dairy allergy at 44. I had to change the sports I played because of the nagging knee injuries I suffered as a teen. I've noticed that I need to write a daily to-do list because I forget things. Not that my memory is going, but I find myself busier than ever, so there's a lot more to do during my day than in previous decades.

I notice I burn very easily, whereas, in my youth, the sun would never bother me. I build up more plaque and tartar on my teeth, so I have to clean my teeth more often. I have seasonal allergies. The pollen in the spring and fall bother me, whereas they never did when I was young. I can't eat carbs too much because I tend to gain weight and feel lethargic when I do. I can't drink alcohol like I used to. I'm now a lightweight and can only handle two drinks when I go out with my friends, or I suffer the consequences for days afterward. I notice I scar easier if I get cut, whether my scab stays on or doesn't.

Physical Myths

"To keep the body in good health is a duty. Otherwise we shall not be able to keep the mind strong and clear." – Buddha

---

* Disclaimer: To be clear, this chapter is not giving you medical advice. Before you begin using any of these ideas, supplements, or therapies, it's always important to seek the guidance and supervision of an expert physician.

As science progresses, we have found out a lot about how our bodies work. Of course, our beliefs about our physical health also change over time. One of the most significant discoveries about the human body came in 2003 when the human genome was finally sequenced. This spurred millions and millions of dollars into gene-altering therapies to help treat and eliminate diseases and mutations in the human body.

There are a lot of myths we have come to think are true about our health which have been learned and studied to be detrimental to our longevity.

Myth #1 "Sleep doesn't matter."

Sleep is one of the most important things we can do for our bodies. There are a lot of processes that occur during sleep. Brain cells reorganize data. Cells restore energy and also go through autophagy. Autophagy is one of the most important processes the body does during sleep. It's the process of breaking down old damaged cells. There are billions and billions of cells in our bodies that make up our tissues and muscles. Each of those cells also has parts that wear out and die. Where do all of these parts go when they wear out and die? Your body can break down these dead cells and recycle their parts to create new parts, and during sleep is an easy time for your body to do this.

During sleep, your body doesn't need to concentrate on logical thinking. It doesn't need to move. It only needs to complete basic functions. So during this time, it can concentrate on removing dead cells and toxins from your body so it can function properly over the long term. So sleep is a very important amount of time you need to give your body to clean up and recycle. Experts recommend seven to eight hours every night for adults and even more for children. If you're physically active, sleeping more hours per night will help your body perform better.

Myth #2 "Breakfast is the most important meal of the day."

Studies back in the 1940s showed that intermittent fasting in animals helped to extend their lifespans. Restricting eating during certain windows of the day has been clinically found to burn fat and lose weight. During this fasting period, the body depletes its carbohydrate stores and starts burning fat instead. If you pair intermittent fasting with a low carbohydrate diet, your body can go into fat-burning mode faster, trimming the pounds of weight from your body.

Many religions fast for certain periods, connecting them with God as a common practice. Author David Asprey writes in *Fast This Way*, "Hunger is a biological message and is something you can control. Craving is a psychological need and is something that tries to control you." During the fasting period, your body goes into survival mode, breaking down anything it can get its hands on to create energy to maintain normal body functions, including normal brain activity.

It's been seen to be a great idea to reset the normal daily metabolic habits your body develops over time with some periods of intermittent fasting. In everything in life, clutter must be eliminated to make room for other things. This same theory holds true for our bodies.

Just like sleep, periods of fasting can help the body break down fat storage that it's been saving as a primal survival instinct. 14-16 hour fasting periods help to reset the body's metabolism so that it isn't always in abundance mode. It can kick it into survival mode. David Asprey also recommends fasting 24 hours once a week to help reset the body. This is a very easy thing to accomplish because we all have busy schedules and work long hours. Once a week, make Mondays your fasting days. Why not? Everyone already hates Mondays. We've all had great weekends. Why not start the week off by doing something good for the body.

Myth #3 "Milk does a body good."

If you ever watch Saturday morning television, you will usually see commercials with surgery cereals and big bowls of milk consumed for breakfast. The thought in the 80s when I was growing up was that daily consumption of milk provided essential vitamins and minerals like calcium, phosphorus, magnesium, and vitamin D, which helped our bodies rebuild bone and muscle.

Fast forward to 2023, and the thought of a daily intake of dairy products, in general, has completely changed. Recent studies by the Physicians' Committee for Responsible Medicine have shown that dairy products, in general, are not very healthy. They are the top source of saturated fats, which can lead to heart disease, type 2 diabetes, and Alzheimer's disease.

According to their research, over 68% of the world's population has lactose malabsorption. So the old adage that milk is good for you is false. Dairy products can also increase the body's inflammatory system, which can be linked to an increase in breast, ovarian, and prostate cancers. Dairy alternatives such as almond, oat, and soy milk can help consumers create the same culinary experience that dairy can without negative connotations.

Myth #4 "If you exercise, you can eat what you want."

Our individual metabolism determines how we break down the foods we eat. Our bodies may burn more calories than our best friend's, yet they may work out more than we do. Have you ever been around someone that could eat whatever they wanted, and yet they were very skinny? Their body has a higher metabolic rate than normal. Then you've also been around people that are grossly overweight even though they watch what they eat.

To stay healthy, we must become very aware of how our body uses the food we give it. If we find that excessive sugar and carbohydrates make us gain weight, then we must avoid those kinds of foods and provide lots of proteins and fats for our bodies to use as fuel.

That's all food is. It's fuel for our body to use to repair itself and use it as energy so we can live our life and enjoy the activities we want. Just because you're working out every day doesn't mean you can eat anything you want and still give your body what it needs. There are countless examples of athletes in their 40s that run every day but die of heart attacks. Sometimes we push ourselves too hard, and our bodies react with a sudden and oftentimes fatal response.

Learning what your body needs and giving it those particular food sources will optimize its performance and give it the longevity we all want. Food and supplementation are the key components to a healthy body. Regular blood work can help to identify what your body is lacking, and then a change in your eating or supplementation regime can be done.

Myth #5 "Weight training makes you huge and bulky."

Most women think that they will become bulky if they start weight training. But weight training helps not only strengthen muscles, but it also can help to maintain a healthy weight. Large muscle groups burn calories; the more active your large main muscle groups are, the more calories they will burn.

Lifting weights can also put pressure on our bones, increasing our bone density. This can help all of us the older we get. If osteoporosis is an issue in your family genetics, weight and strength training can help to ensure your bone density maintains normal levels.

Besides our physical demands on our bodies, we also have mental and spiritual demands we must deal with. Patience, karma, attitudes, thoughts, beliefs, and goals are all realms of our health we have to deal with and improve for our physical bodies to perform optimally.

Mental

Mental health is just as important as physical health. If our mentality is positive, healthy, caring, and growing, our physical world will reflect the same.

Connection

"Connection is why we're here. It is what gives purpose and meaning to our lives." – Brene Brown

---

One of our six basic needs is love and connection. We all need to feel that we belong to our family and community. It is imperative that we find people that love us and support us so that we can grow and become the best versions of ourselves. I am writing this book at a time when people are starting to question their identities and where they fit in our society. The sad part is that they don't realize their uniqueness makes them great. Their uniqueness expands society's awareness and tests the norms and cliches that keep our communities and civilizations from progressing toward freedom of expression.

LBGTQ+. The Woke. Conservatives. Progressives. African Americans. Latinos. Caucasians. Asians. It really doesn't matter what identity we believe we are. What matters is that everyone has the right to identify and act as they wish. But it also doesn't mean that another's way of thinking and living has any domain over yours. Right now, in America, people's free speech, our first Amendment rights are being questioned and silenced by mainstream media and agenda-driven social media companies. Shame on them! We have men competing in women's sports because they identify as women. Shame on them! There are reasons that physical women compete against physical women, so it's a level playing field. Just because someone has a different opinion than you gives them absolutely no right to infringe their opinion on you or try to silence yours.

Being an American means that we as a society are free to pursue our lives as we see fit and not believe that our way of doing things is the only way. That's communism and Marxism, and it has no room in America for this kind of thinking. We must rise above all the propaganda and use our uniqueness and God-given talents to work together to fix our world's problems. Don't we all want this? Unfortunately, right now, that's not the case.

If you want to grow and contribute, you must first learn how to work with other people. You must learn how to communicate with others in a way that they not only understand you but also believe in what you're saying. That doesn't mean you're trying to convert them to your beliefs or infringing on their free thoughts. But it means you must find a common ground you can all agree upon and go from there.

This takes work and creativity. It also takes a lot of patience and willingness to admit when you're wrong. I have been wrong about many things during my life so far, and I've also been right about many things. I have learned that any success or failure that has come into my life thus far has all started with me and my thoughts at the time.

Something that has become rampant in this country is fear. The media scared everyone when Covid-19 happened in 2020. It started spreading like wildfire, and millions worldwide became infected by it. The first wave of Covid was strong and deadly to a lot of people in the population. But as it spread throughout the world, different strains appeared and increased its infectious ability while decreasing its strength and deadliness.

In 2023, Covid-19 is still infectious, but we as a society have started to move on with our lives. We are traveling again. We are doing business in person again. We are working in the office again. We are behaving like we did before the pandemic occurred. This is a good thing. We are not as fearful as a society as we were a couple of years ago.

In any bad situation, humans tend to go through stages of grief. First, they go through denial. Like with Covid-19 or a job loss or a death, we can't believe it has happened to us or around us. We wish it didn't happen. We sometimes even act like it didn't happen.

Then there's the anger stage. This is where most of us play the victim. Why did this happen? Why did this happen to me? Why am I so unlucky? I think in America right now, we're in the anger stage. We're mad about slavery, something that was fought against and stifled over 100 years ago. We're mad about enormous inflation, something that is logical considering Covid-19 shut down large factories and disrupted supply chains around the world. We're mad about people expressing themselves, even though they have every right according to the Bill of Rights.

For society to move on and for people to connect again, we need to go through the third stage: bargaining. We need to find common ground with each other so we can help each other make the most of our lives. We need to compromise. We need to listen. We need to empathize with the other side and question our own beliefs to see if they are truly our own or those that others have passed down to us.

We then can go through the next phase: depression. We can certainly feel sorry for ourselves and feel like everyone, and everything is against us. But we must ask ourselves, is this true? Is every single person and every single occurrence around us against us? We may find no way out or a light at the end of the tunnel. But if we can turn on the rational, educated, objective part of our mind and turn down our emotions, we can come to the last stage: acceptance. We don't have to see acceptance as losing or being broken down. We can see acceptance as something that we can let go of and move on from.

No matter how bad our lives get. No matter what obstacles come between us and our dreams, we must believe that we can go through them and live in a free and accepting society. This all starts with our mentality. This all starts with detaching ourselves from popular media and companies with agendas. We must ask ourselves if we should be treating other people like this. We should ask ourselves if other people should have the right to treat us like this when we know they certainly do not.

Belief

"We have always held to the hope, the belief, the conviction that there is a better life, a better world, beyond the horizon."- Franklin D Roosevelt

---

Our mental toughness and willpower is the only thing that can push us beyond our boundaries. Beyond our comfort zones. Our creativity, perseverance, and imagination can propel us further and further in our human experience. But we must guard our minds. We must protect it against the poisonous ridicule, opinions, and political agenda of the outside world. One person can completely change a society. One person can help another person. One person can create a product or service to revolutionize the human experience. One person can break a record not believed to be broken in the past.

Anything is possible. Anything can happen if we keep fear and negativity out of our minds and souls. It's not about perfection; it's about progress. How can we advance our society with our contributions and talents? How can we improve our lives and communities to live better lives?

I personally have been reading a lot of philosophy over the past two years. It is fascinating that people 2,000 years ago went through similar problems, events, and situations that I find myself in thousands of years later. We all love each other. We all suffer loss. We all care about our family and friends. We all work and contribute to our communities. We all help each other. Sometimes things work out for us. Sometimes they don't, but in the end, our human experiences are very similar. Whether it's the Stoics, the Christians, or the Buddhists, we can take a glance at the similarities and differences in our lives when we read books from people living during these times. We can also experience their thoughts and mental perspective of what they were going through at the time.

What I've gotten out of these writings is that we're all the same. I may be as unique as a snowflake. But my life and the things I go through during it are not unique, and the people that went before me have the wisdom to learn and implement in my life to help me navigate triumphs and strife.

In many cultures, their elder members are sought for wisdom and are celebrated. In other cultures, they are shunned as if they have nothing to contribute anymore. This is a travesty and should stop immediately. So many things have happened in the last 50 years that anyone who has survived and thrived during this time can help contribute wisdom and practicality to our communities. Listen to them. Learn from them. Implement things that have helped them succeed during their lives. Heed their warnings. Celebrate in their paths. They've lived through it and can help us all wade through the weeds that come up in our own journeys through life.

One theme that propagates throughout the ancient writings is hope. Hope for a better tomorrow. Hope for happiness. Hope for unity. This gives a message of positivity to everyone that wants it. We can wallow in the misery that befalls us or believe in hope and know that, in time, things will pass. As in time, nothing stays the same. Everything can change if we want them to. We can break out of poverty. We can persevere through an obstacle that's in our way. We can work daily on our goals and dreams to create the life we truly want, no matter our current situation.

To improve, we must first start with our beliefs. We must first believe that we are worthy of happiness, health, and success. Then we must change the things that we accept. If our standards change, our lives can change. We must learn the skills necessary to earn more money if we want more money. We must study and practice what the wealthy do and implement these skills into our lives. We must stop accepting poverty and the poverty ways of thinking.

If we want better health. We must believe that we can be healthy and learn the skills that the healthy have and start implementing those actions. We must change our diets. We must change the way we move our bodies. We must stop accepting poor health habits and unhealthy ways of thinking.

We must first visualize our dreams, learn how to achieve them, and act on them. Thoughts, skills, and actions. This is the true formula for success in every area of our lives. But it all starts in our minds. It all starts with our thinking and our general attitude. If we truly want something to change, we must first believe that it's possible for us and that we can achieve it no matter where we're starting.

As they say, "Talk is cheap; results beat conversation every day." This is a very true statement. But sometimes that's a tall order. There will always be obstacles in our way; sometimes, our struggles and obstacles are different from others. But in the end, no obstacle is too big for one to overcome. No obstacle. We must see past the obstacle and only focus on what we truly want.

As I trained in martial arts, we often would practice breaking through wood. The practice wasn't about breaking through wood; it was a mental exercise of visualization, belief, and actualization. They taught us to visualize hitting through the other end of the board to either the divide holding the board or the actual instructor on the other end. We would focus our attention on the spot on the other end of the board, breathe deep, and then shout loudly as we struck the board. For me, this was a very easy exercise because I had mentally trained myself to visualize my results for decades. But for others, it was not an easy exercise. They saw the wood as an actual physical obstacle in the way of achieving their goal. I never saw it as an obstacle at all. All I could visualize was hitting the spot on the other side of the wood, not the wood itself. Because I visualized my goal, I could easily achieve it.

This is the same exercise that can be used in any area of life. Instead of focusing on the obstacles that are in the way of achieving your goals, just focus on the goal itself. The obstacles will fall away when they have no power over you. Write down your goals on paper every day. Read them aloud every day. This will bring them from your mind into the physical world. Then act on those goals and only focus on you achieving them. It's mind over matter. What you don't mind doesn't matter. Get it? Only focus on what you want. Never focus on what you don't want. That's the prescription for success.

Hobbies

" Hobbies are great distractions from the worries and troubles that plague daily living." - Bill Malone

---

Activities that can combine physical, mental, and spiritual health are hobbies. Whether it's playing golf, playing chess, or meditating, hobbies can help to enrich our lives for the better.

Most hobbies involve other people. Sometimes they are competitive and evoke physical and mental prowess. Other times, they are quiet and creative, like writing or knitting. Some activities we can do throughout our lives, while others are only for the youth and active. But that's okay. As long as we enjoy these activities, their benefits outweigh their competitiveness.

Finding activities that you enjoy is very important. Hobbies can give you a creative outlet. Many amateur painters and musicians enjoy the creativity of their art, even though they may not be the best artist or musicians in the world. Amateurs don't care. They love their activities, and they spend their resources enjoying them.

It's a release for them. Almost a spiritual awakening that happens when they use their talent to make something that no one else can make. Whether it's cooking a delicious meal or playing an original song, hobbies can help to trigger our sleeping creativity and inner originality. We are all truly unique like the snowflakes that fall during a winter storm or a petal of a flower that stretches out to catch the sunlight through a cloud. We are all truly unique and should embrace that uniqueness when we get the chance.

Hobbies can be one of the ways we embrace that uniqueness. Maybe you have a helluva strike with your 3 wood on a narrow fairway. Maybe you can whip up a delicious meal with only a few ingredients. It doesn't matter *what* talents you have, only that you *express* them consistently.

I love to learn about my inner thoughts. About spirituality. About running my business. I love music even though I can't play a note. I love to create videos and edit them, even though I know they are very amateurish. I love cooking even though I don't have as much time to devote to proper training. I still do it and enjoy trying new recipes every chance I get. I love to write and have made it a daily activity. I have put these things in my calendar as an event or task to incorporate them into my daily life.

What do you enjoy doing? What activity lights you up when you are doing it? What would you enjoy doing if you had all the money, time, and energy in the world? That's your hobby. That's the activity or activities you should pursue. That's the hobby that can make you happy from within. That can light you up. That can drive you. That can relieve your everyday stress. That's the

God-given talent that you should pursue and enjoy. And it doesn't matter if you make any money from it. It doesn't matter if it's any good. It doesn't even matter if anyone ever sees it. As long as it lights you up and brings out your creativity, strength, and uniqueness, then that's the hobby you should enjoy in your daily life.

Spiritual

"Remember, we are not human beings having a spiritual experience. We are spiritual beings having a human experience."
-Stephen Covey

Our spiritual health is very important. We want to feel the connection not only with other people but also with something bigger than ourselves. For some people, this may mean religion. For others, this may mean living their lives with purpose and meaning. Charity. Contribution. Making a difference. All of these things can help to connect us with other people.

When we first start out in life, we're very selfish. It's all about our dreams and goals. But once we achieve the goals and dreams we want, we may find a lack of meaning behind those goals and dreams. It becomes more than just ourselves. It can drive us to be part of the human collective.

As we will talk about later in the book, relationships are very important to living a sustained life. But it also helps bring meaning to it too. How often have you achieved a goal, an award, or even a compliment and immediately thought of a loved one to share it with? We, as humans, strive for connection. We strive for progress and a sense of expansion. But when we progress and expand, we want our environment and the people we spend the most time with to progress and expand with us. Sometimes this happens, and sometimes it doesn't.

Throughout life, you will realize that everyone and everything has a finite place in your time horizon. Some people in your life will slowly fade because they're not growing in the direction you are. Some dreams and goals that you once thought were of the utmost importance at one time suddenly start fading away because your priorities change. This is okay. This is normal. This is called the life journey.

Religion points to the assumption that we are created in God's image. That humans are made from the divine. Whether this is true or not, we have to ask ourselves the bigger picture, "What are we doing here? What is our purpose?" We could go down many rabbit holes, and many theologians and philosophers have done that through the centuries. But I want to ask you to simply find what the meaning of your life is for you.

What are you meant to do in a broad sense? Are you a teacher? Are you a martyr? Are you a record breaker? Are you a great thinker? Are you a problem solver? There's really only a handful of categories your life could fall into.

For me, I am a teacher. I soak up information from various sources and use that information to form practical advice to help other people. And it's not just advice; it's information I've applied in my life. Thus, this advice has experience and practical conclusions behind it.

I have lived through all of these subjects in this book in my five decades on this planet. Living through the Information Age has shattered many thoughts and beliefs about myself and the world we live in. It has truly reshaped my life, and it will do the same for you. But you have to be open to it. You have to open your mind and allow different ideas and ways of living to penetrate your consciousness.

You can only do two things with a new idea: accept it and make it a part of your existence or reject it and keep living the way you've always been living. Information is just that. It's facts or opinions. It's objective or subjective. What you do with this information can either change your life or keep it the same way. The truth about information is that it can open up a new way of thinking, living, doing things, thought, and belief. Isn't that what human existence is about?

We live in a civilized world. But this doesn't mean we can't change. We can't evolve. We can't make things better. There are so many things that are wrong with the world we live in. Pollution. Bigotry. Abuse. War. Poverty. Starvation.

But think about how many good things we've discovered and have improved? The world is a smaller place than it used to be. We are more aware of the problems and of the technology and science that can help solve those problems like never before. We are slowly closing the gap between wealth and poverty, of mindsets, health, and ethnicities.

We are slowly backing up ancient spiritual beliefs with modern science. We are learning and transforming the way we think about ourselves and the world we live in.

We are evolving. We are growing. We are getting better. Our thoughts are advancing, and scientific and technological advances are being made. These advances are slowly being incorporated into our everyday lives and helping us be better humans.

We are learning how our thoughts can become things in the physical world. What a marvelous and wondrous time we live in! And it all starts with you and me.

One person can certainly make a difference. You can create a chain of change that can affect so many people's lives. Giving, helping, and creating. These are all gifts from God and the Universe. No matter how religious you are, you must admit that there's something out there, a universal power that ties us all together. There's something out there that gives us that new idea. There's something out there that allows us to feel love. There's something out there that gives us the ambition to try again. To persevere when all hope is gone. To try again when everything is against us. And this is where your spirituality begins. This is where your journey begins.

We get so caught up in our everyday mundane routines that we forget to work on our spiritual side. To give ourselves a break from the noisy everyday chaos that follows us around. Especially if we're working. Especially if we're parents. Time can fly past us, and we can forget to work on this part of ourselves that is vital to our lives. Spirituality. Belief. Strength. Ambition. Perseverance. These are all things that come from within. These are all things that must be nurtured so that when times get tough, we can endure them.

Take some time every day to be grateful. Take some time to look at old family photos and remember those days. Take some time to call someone you haven't talked to in a while. Spend some time reading something that will challenge your beliefs about yourself and humankind. It's this time during the day that will become your favorite. It's this time during the day that you can connect with your true self and can build the strength to endure what lies ahead of you. Reflect. Be grateful. Open your mind to new ideas and thoughts and improve the things you discover about yourself that you want to change. Grow. Contribute. Improve. Progress. This is what life truly is about. Becoming a better person, not only for yourself but for others in your life.

When you do this, you will feel fulfilled. Your body will release serotonin which will make your body feel satisfied. This can, in turn, decrease the amount of cortisol in your body and can help relieve stress and anxiety. Having gratitude and feeling a positive attitude can help your body deal with any obstacle that comes its way. Being mentally strong with a body ready for the challenge can put you on the road to success.

Chapter 7

Intention

"Every why hath a wherefore."–William Shakespeare

In 2021, the average male lived around 69.8 years. For a female, it's 72.56 years. That's around 840 months, 3640 weeks, 25,550 days, 613,200 hours, or 36,792,000 minutes. It doesn't sound like a lot of time. Does it? How long does the average person spend watching TV per day? According to the A.C. Nielsen Co., the average American watches more than four hours of TV daily (or 28 hours/week, or two months of non-stop TV-watching per year). In a 65-year life, that person will have spent nine years glued to the tube.

An average person spends 145 minutes daily on social media, or 2 hours and 25 minutes daily.

How long does the average person sleep? Most adults need seven to nine hours of sleep each day.

So let's look at how we spend our day. 24 hours.

8 hours = sleeping

8 hours = working

4 hours = watching TV

2 ½ hours = looking at social media

1 ½ hours = eating, doing chores or homework, working out.

That's clearly not enough time to get everything else done *and* enjoy our lives *and* grow as a person. It's so easy to get distracted. With 200+ cable channels on your TV, many social media outlets spewing new content at you every minute, and new meet-ups and organizations that ask for your resources around every corner. It's no wonder why all of us feel stressed and out of energy. We are required to make thousands of small decisions every day, which takes up a lot of mental energy. This same energy that can be spent on things that truly matter to us: our families, friends, and life goals.

Does it really matter what shenanigans the Kardashians are up to? Should I really care that there's a new iPhone on the market that does the same thing the last five models have done? Hey, Apple, Steve Jobs is dead. You'd better come up with some new innovations because the public is getting tired of the same old stuff!

What happened to a leisurely late-night dinner with your friends? What happened to a slow romantic walk with your honey? What happened to spending some time with your child looking up at the stars and wishing you could touch one? What happened to all of these things that I myself grew up with? It's called technology; that's what happened. We are allowing the "machines" to take over our lives. Now's the time that we take them back!

To do this, we must live with intention. We must figure out our goals for our families and what is important to us. I know it's easier said than done, but it's possible and a must. When you are traveling with your GPS and have the exact address, do you follow the map laid out in front of you? Of course, you do. If you accidentally turn down the wrong street, the GPS will still find a different way to get you there, even if that means you have to turn around and go back to the original route. Your goals and intentions are your GPS for living the life you want to live.

Time

"Time waits for no man."- Proverb from St. Mahrer

If you want to spend more time with your kids, friends, or spouse, you must clear your schedule of things that get in the way of your objective. If you want to lose weight, you must clear out the junk food in your pantry and fridge. If you want to save and invest more money, you have to budget your money and tell it where to go. Living with intention is simple to do but not necessarily easy.

I get it; you want to give your kids the life you may or may not have had. You want to give them the best. But does this mean that to give them the "best," you must work two jobs so you can buy them the "thing" that you *thought* they wanted but didn't really want or need? Most kids want to have fun. And that fun usually involves you. They want to spend time with you. They want to have fun with you. They want to experience new things with you. They want to learn from you. They simply want time. That's it. Simple, right? But this is where our time needs to become a priority. Our time needs to be budgeted, too, as well as our other resources.

It's okay to say no to the things that will mess up our time budget. It's okay to allow other people to make the cupcakes for the PTA meeting, volunteer to clean up after the party or drive extra kids to practice. You don't have to feel guilty because you have made a time budget, and these extra things aren't on the schedule.

We must stop comparing our life to others. We must stop thinking that we must do fifty different things during the day because our mom did that for us when we were young. We need to realize that life was simpler when we were growing up. Heck, I had a corded phone and no internet when I was growing up. We had to use our imaginations and go outside and play during the day. It's okay if you fall short on things. But if you live with intention, you'll be able to prioritize how you're spending your time, and you'll be able to get things done that are important to you with no regrets.

The one thing you can't get back is your time. We can buy time by hiring other people to clean our houses, mow our lawns, and grocery shop. But there are still only 24 hours in a day, and we must prioritize how we spend those 24 hours. If you cut out the TV and the social media crap, you can gain nearly 25% back of your day. Think about what you can accomplish with an extra 6 ½ hours every day? The possibilities are endless!

The Roman philosopher Seneca said it well in a letter to Paulinus: "It is not that we have a short space of time, but that we waste much of it. Life is long enough, and it has been given in sufficiently generous measure to allow the accomplishment of the very greatest things if the whole of it is well invested. But when it is squandered in luxury and carelessness, when it is devoted to no good end, forced at last by the ultimate necessity we perceive that it has passed away before we were aware that it was passing. So it is—the life we receive is not short, but we make it so, nor do we have any lack of it, but are wasteful of it."

The older you get, you'll realize that you must conserve what energy you do have and use it wisely. You'll have to ask yourself if the activity that's up for question is one you want to use that energy on or not.

According to Greg McKeown, author of *Essentialism, The Disciplined Pursuit of Less,* to get back your time, you must ask yourself a simple question, "Is this the most important thing I should be doing with my time and resources right now?"

If it's not, then why are you doing it? Greg's entire book is about prioritizing your time so that you can live the way of the Essentialist, which is the relentless pursuit of less but better. Greg's not saying that you fill your time doing nothing. He's saying that you fill your schedule with activities that bring value to your life. Value. Not boredom. Not chaos. Living with intention and not allowing anyone or anything that is *not* a priority for you to waste one of your precious resources on.

This includes work activities. How often have you put in a few extra hours helping a colleague on a project that needed to be finished? How many times did you bring work home with you to finish? How many times did your meeting run late, and you missed your kid's baseball game? Unfortunately, most of us have done one or more of these things. What we don't realize is that we don't owe our private life to our work life? In fact, it's the other way around. We only have a work-life to subsidize our private life. This is the way you should look at your job. I know, I know. You may be thinking that I've totally missed the boat here. You may think I don't understand that you love your job or career and that you matter in the workplace. What you do matters.

The question you must ask yourself is whether *you* work your job or if your *job* works for you.

If your job works for you, then now's the time to start being more deliberate with the time you spend at work. It's okay to start turning people down when that activity takes up precious time that you could be spending on something that matters to you and your advancement in the company. It's okay to be selfish here. It's your life. It's okay to be a team player, but it's also okay to be a lone wolf.

It's your life. It's your career. We, as Americans, typically hold ambition over intention. That's why burnout rates are so high in many industries. We tend to forsake our personal lives for opportunities that can result from long hours in the office. I experienced this in my own practice. Many people that work corporate jobs or own their own businesses feel as if they must do everything. They feel that they must work hard and give it their all.

This, of course, is true to a point. It's not that we must give it *all* to our jobs or businesses. I think that's where we make our mistakes. We must give our *best* to our careers, not all of our time and energy. I learned this from a consultant. I learned that I could give my best to my patients without spending all of my time and energy doing it. That was a big shift for me. Learning how to schedule my day so that my goals could be met and having enough time and energy to spend living the rest of my life.

In my own dental practice, I've learned how to take care of my patient load and do it only three days a week. The other four days I spend with my family doing the things *I* want to do. Things like working out, reading, writing my own books and materials, and filming *The Beer Divas* show. I have made it a priority to cut out cable and spend at least one to two hours with my family every day. I have time to cook. I have time to work out. I have time with my honey. I also have time to work on my personal development, which I have made a must since hitting 40.

I don't volunteer at my kid's school. I don't hang out with friends very often. I don't go window shopping. I don't spend time on Facebook or Instagram unless I am posting a video for *The Beer Divas* show. I don't spend my day doing things that don't add value to my life. Plain and simple! And best of all, I don't feel *guilty* about it. I'm a busy person! I own a dental practice, spend time reading and writing, enjoy tasting beers from all around the world, travel from time to time, and hang out with my family. I am doing *exactly* what I want to do.

But it wasn't always like that. The older I get, the more I want to "slow down." It's not that I don't have passion or ambition; it's just that I have learned to prioritize the things that make a difference in my life and allow the other things to fall by the wayside.

It's not important to me that I make cupcakes for my kid's class. It's not important to me to look at Facebook and see all the people I barely know doing things I don't want to do. I don't spend time worrying about what people think of me. My priority is to live with intention and not worry about the rest. Living with intention keeps me pretty busy all by itself. It fills my days with doing things I may not have time to do if I lived my life for other people doing things *they* want me to do. I've also realized that I don't have the energy I once had.

And yes, I know this. And yes, I feel this way also. Not everyone can drill into people's faces and take away the pain or fix their mouth problems like I can. Not everyone could stand doing that. I get it. But what I've learned in my 40s is that I don't owe anyone my expertise when it interferes with my private life. My private life is more important than anything else. I don't care what happens; my private life is sacred and a priority.

This is why I hired a really expensive consultant four years ago to help me rearrange my practice so that I could earn the same amount of money 25% of the time. Prioritizing my time at work gave me freedom of time in my personal life. I'm not on call. I can ask a colleague to help with emergencies when I'm out of town. I have employees who answer the phone on Mondays and Fridays and help with patient care. To me, it's a dream come true.

I'm not *owned* by my practice; I *own* my practice. Yes, I'm still an employee of my practice. But I have more freedom than I did previously and I can set what time I spend in it and what time I don't. It's freedom.

That's what living with intention is about. Learning how to prioritize what's right for you. Learning what's right for you and not sacrificing the people and the things you love. What I had to learn was that it's my business. I can run it any way that I see fit. I can spend as much time and energy in it or out of it as I want to, and no one else's opinions matter. I'm the boss, and I get to decide.

Even if you work for someone else, you're still the boss of your life. You still get to decide how much time and energy you put into your career and private life. I think during these post-Covid times, people realize that they have more power over their lives than they previously believed. Many people are starting their own businesses or finding jobs that align better with their values, which is beautiful.

A useful strategy to help set resource priority is using President Dwight D Eisenhower's "Urgent vs Important" problem determination. During his presidential term, President Eisenhower knew that his time as President was short, but he didn't lack a plethora of things to do every day. He devised a strategy that his staff could employ to categorize his daily agenda. Things were either "urgent" or "important." Sometimes they were both. Sometimes, they were neither.

If they were "important," these problems could lead to personal goal achievement. If they were "urgent," these problems could lead to goal achievement for other people, not necessarily for personal advancement but needed to be addressed immediately.

In our own lives, we can use President Eisenhower's same categories to help us use our time efficiently and effectively. If the task at hand is important, we know we should work on it as much as we can daily until it gets done. If it's unimportant, then we shouldn't waste our time on it. For example, we know that staying healthy is important. If we have a choice of eating a nice healthy salad for lunch or some fast food, what choice will help us achieve staying healthy? Right, eating a salad for lunch. That's an important choice that helps us achieve our goal of health and longevity.

What if your son just fell off his bike and cut up his knee? This, of course, is not only important, you must stop the bleeding and clean his wound, but also urgent. It needs to be done right now. This would require your time immediately to help your son.

But what if a task is urgent but not really important? This usually is mundane office work or personal chores that should be done but seem like they need to be done right now. The question to ask yourself is, "Do I have any *important* things to do before I use my time for this *urgent* task?" Importance *always* comes before urgent unless it's an emergency. If all of the important things are done, then the urgent mundane tasks can be accomplished.

Using President Eisenhower's important versus urgent categorization, you can better control your time allocation. You can prioritize what's important to you and your family and work on the important things you want to accomplish in your life. If it's important to you, you should do it. If it's important to others, you can do it only *after* you've done what's important to you.

Living with intention over time also warrants us to be efficient and effective. Being efficient is doing the task in the least amount of time and effort. Effectiveness is getting the job done in the least steps possible. They go hand in hand. If we rush to get a task done, we falter, and having to do it again isn't efficient or effective. We may have accomplished the task, but we used more resources to get the job done. Sometimes simple isn't easy. Sometimes fast isn't fast if it means not being efficient and effective.

Both efficiency and effectiveness intertwine with time. British historian Cyril Northcote Parkinson termed his phrase "Parkinson's Law." It states, " Work expands to fill the time available for its completion."

Have you ever had an assignment due in a week but didn't get it done until the last possible moment? Why? We habitually learn how long our projects will take us to complete. Most of us can complete the project in a certain amount of time. When someone gives us more time, we tend to lengthen the time it takes for us to complete the project, even though we subconsciously know it will only take a shorter time frame to complete the project. Most of us will wait until the last minute to start and complete the project. The only way to cut out Parkinson's Law is to set a firmer timeline for the project or goal to be completed.

With a shorter time frame in the balance, greater efficiency and effectiveness techniques come to the forefront. Pareto's Law of 80/20 comes into effect. We know that 80% of the successful outcomes come from doing 20% of action steps. We can become more efficient and effective in task completion by eliminating the 80% of actions, thoughts, and people that won't help us complete the task at hand. Once this technique is perfected, then the virus of distraction must be addressed. How do we eliminate distractions and the tendency for procrastination?

In the late 1980s, Francesco Cirillo was a struggling college student. He was having a difficult time not only focusing on his studies but also getting his projects completed on time. He used a tomato kitchen timer and challenged himself to work on an assignment due in ten minutes. He set the timer and worked undistracted on that assignment for the next ten minutes. His logic was that ten minutes wasn't too long to concentrate on a task. By shortening the time required to avoid distraction, he could start to break down any complicated task into simple action steps he could take simultaneously, thus achieving his end goal of completion. He named this the Pomodoro effect after the tomato kitchen timer.

Later, the technique was lengthened to 25-minute increments with a short five-minute break between the 25-minute focus sessions. In the November 2003 issue of ACM's Queue, Jakob Nielsen raised interesting questions surrounding the concept of "information pollution." In his essay, Nielsen said, "A one-minute interruption can easily cost a knowledge worker 10 to 15 minutes of lost productivity due to the time needed to reestablish mental context and reenter the flow state."

It's this *flow state* that we're looking for. When we're in this flow state, our concentration is heightened, our frontal lobe, which is in charge of problem-solving, fires profusely, and time is of no importance to us. Have you ever started on a project, looked at the clock, and realized you hadn't eaten for the day? It's now dark, and everyone at the office is gone. But you were so engrossed in your project that your awareness was only on your project and not the environment around you.

That's the flow state. That's spending your time intentionally. Whether using President Eisenhower's important versus urgent strategy, Parkinson's Law, or the Pomodoro technique, creating the life you want is possible. You can get everything you want done once you prioritize what's important and eliminate the rest of the distractions that keep you from achieving it.

Money

"You will either learn to manage money, or the lack of it will manage you."– Dave Ramsey

We can continue this theme of prioritizing our lives into the subject of money. How can we live intentionally with money? Again, this is a very simple concept, but not necessarily easy to accomplish.

I think the Covid pandemic of 2020 stopped people in their same-old-routine tracks. People spent more time at home because it was unsafe to travel. Many people were sent home to work and had to juggle their resources while managing their children. I think it was a blessing to most. Not in the sense that millions were getting sick and even dying. That's not what I'm saying. I think it was a blessing to most because it made them look at their lives and really start to think about what was important and necessary to them.

During the pandemic, some people lost their jobs. These people soon realized what things were important to them. They had to cut out a lot of things. They had to sell some things to have some extra cash. They had to ask for help from the government or their creditors because they got caught with their pants down, so to speak!

During this time, I was definitely caught with my pants down and realized that my dental practice was closed. Yikes! I had a little money saved in the bank, but I had just made a large investment into real estate two months prior and overextended our bank accounts. I had a few panicked nights worrying about how I would pay for our mortgage, food, and all of my other obligations. What about my dental practice rent and utilities?

Being a person that never acted like a victim, I took matters into my own hands. The first order of business was to get my finances right, but where to start? In my YouTube feed, a Dave Ramsey video came up. I never watched any of his videos nor listened to any of his podcasts, but I decided to see what he had to say. That was one of the most important steps I took to get my life back on track.

Love him or hate him, Dave knows how to get out of debt and spend with intention. Dave teaches you about the baby steps. I don't want to get into those, as he can tell you better than I do, but the first order of business was to get myself on a budget. I always had some extra money and no credit card debt. But I soon realized I had too many obligations to creditors for dental equipment, mortgages, and cars. Dave mentions Proverbs 22:7, which states:

"The rich rule over the poor, and the borrower is a slave to the lender."

I'm not a religious person, per se, but this really summed up how I felt. My main income streams from my dental practice and my real estate had dried up, yet all of my creditors were asking for the money I owed them. Luckily, my husband was still working, so he and his business handled basic utilities and food.

I realized that I needed to be more intentional with my money and tell it where to go. I realized how important a written budget was to accomplishing everything I wanted to do with my money. I downloaded Dave's free app, Every Dollar, and got to work after my practice reopened.

After filling in the budget, I realized I had an extra $300 a week left over. I decided to use that money to build up my emergency fund of three months' worth of expenses. That took me to the end of 2020. After that, I wanted to tackle my only remaining personal debt over my head: the mortgage. I used all of the extra money to start winding down the mortgage. I had six years left on my 15-year mortgage, one of the few money-related decisions that were a great one. I told my husband that we were going to tackle this large endeavor.

Was toilet paper necessary? Maybe. I'll never forget my husband went out to hunt and gather- that's what he loves to do. He went to Sam's Club and Giant Eagle and brought back a full carload of stuff. Canned goods. Toilet paper for an entire year. Meat that could be frozen in our extra freezers. He told me that if shit was going down, we would be prepared. He even bought an AR-15 rifle and as much ammo as he could find. I know, maybe a little unnecessary, but he wanted to make sure we were okay, and of course, I love him for his Boy Scout preparedness.

During 2021, I said no a lot, especially to my kid. But I always followed my no with a reason. Being ten years old, he seemed to understand that a little sacrifice now would lead to more fun and more freedom later. It took me the entire year of 2021 to pay off that mortgage. But I have to say it feels amazing!

What a relief I feel now that I can concentrate my money on retirement and having fun along the way. I feel that huge weight off my back. I feel better prepared for what life has for me in the future. All of this by doing a simple little budget.

Once my practice was up and running again, I decided to do the same for the dental practice. I looked at all of my bills and started cutting products and services that weren't necessary. I used my PPP money to help my staff and to keep the practice going. When I didn't use all of the PPP money, I put it into a savings account and didn't touch it. This was the start of my business emergency fund, which I had never done before.

Once the public was vaccinated, our practice numbers started booming to pre-covid levels. Money started rolling in, and our budget was so tight by the end of 2021 that I paid off almost all of my business debt.

So now I have a lot of wiggle room, both personally and professionally. It took the pandemic for me to get my money right and to spend it with intention. I had to ask myself, "Is this service or product worthy of my hard-earned money?" Most of the time, the answer was no.

Are you living intentionally with your money? If you're in credit card debt, have a mortgage, and live paycheck to paycheck, then the answer is no. Most of us aren't taught this either at school or at home. Most of our parents have no clue how to be intentional with their money. Have you asked yourself on Monday, "I just got paid on Friday, and where did all my money go?" If so, you're allowing money to flow out of your life without discretion instead of telling it what to do. That's what a budget is for.

The Minimalist Joshua Fields Millburn asks himself these questions before making any purchases:

1. Who am I buying this for?

2. Will this add value to my life?

3. Can I afford it?

4. Is this the best use of this money?

5. What's the *actual* cost?

6. Would the best version of me buy this?

Let's dive into these questions:

"Who am I buying this for?" This question refers to peer pressure. Are you buying this thing to impress people you don't know or people who don't care? Are you buying this thing to make you feel happy? Do you want it, or do you need it?

"Will this add value to my life?" Is this something that will create time, energy, or money for you? I know that if my vacuum cleaner breaks, I will need another one because I like a clean house and hate to use the broom. So a vacuum cleaner will add value to my everyday life and my cleanliness. If you want a new pair of boots but already have 20 other pairs of boots, will this new pair really add more value to your life?

"Can I afford it?" We'll talk later about doing a budget and identifying where all of your money is going. The only way to have a healthy financial life is to manage our money wisely. And that's knowing exactly where our money is going. If you need to make payments on a couch, you can't afford it! If you need to cash in your 401k to buy that house, you can't afford it. If you need to take out a Payday loan, you certainly can't afford it!

"Is this the best use of this money?" If you want those new pair of boots but still have $6,000 worth of credit card debt, then using this money to buy this new pair of boots you don't need will probably be a poor choice. If you need a new pair of boots for work because your old ones are worn out and making your feet hurt, then this is a wise decision with your money. But if you have consumer debt, you need to concentrate on using your money to pay off the debt you owe other people for things you've purchased in the past. Get caught up on your consumerism!

"What's the *actual* cost?" The actual cost of something is not just in monetary value. You still have to maintain, repair, store, and use it. That costs time, money, and effort. Can you afford the actual cost of this thing to maintain it over the long haul?

"Would the best version of me buy this?" If you're living with intention, does this purchase follow this intention? If you will use this thing and it brings value to you, then it's okay. If you're in debt and owe others for everything, this purchase is not helping you become debt free and more intentional with your money.

These questions are a big help when it comes to deciding whether you want to make a purchase or not. For me, I know that I need to tell my money where to go. If the item in question is not on my budget list, I must ask myself these questions to decide if this purchase is right for me.

I keep using the word "budget." I know most people hate the word "budget." But all a budget is is a plan for where you want your money to go. It helps with impulse purchases and intentionally keeps you and your money out of trouble. I know I will never go a month without budgeting that month. My budget ensures that I'm saving to invest, that my bills are paid off, and that I have money to spend how I want to. I know that I can have fun as long as it's listed in my budget, and it keeps me from making money mistakes.

Holidays and birthdays are planned out ahead of time. There's always money sitting aside for those important things like vacations, home improvements, and school supplies. If you know Christmas is around the corner, start budgeting ahead of time and set aside money, so you have it when you need it.

According to Dave Ramsey's website, if you charge $1048 on your 17% APR credit card and only make the minimum $25 a month payment on that card, it would take you a whopping five years to pay it off and would cost you another $553 in interest payments. So that $1000 Christmas costs you 50% more if it takes you more time to pay it off. And guess what? You still have next year's Christmas to contend with, and so on and so forth. When will this madness ever stop?

If you set aside money every month during the year, you never have to put it on a charge card again. That's what a budget is for. It allows you to plan where your money's going so you don't wake up and wonder where it all went. With a budget, you know exactly where it went and have 100% control over your budget plan. Money loves to have direction; if you can be intentional with it and control your impulses, you can live your life knowing that you always have money for what you want to experience.

If you want to go on vacation, you can budget for that. If you want a new pair of boots, you can budget for that. If you want a new car, you can also budget for that ahead of time to pay cash and save money on the loan interest. A budget doesn't constrict you; it allows you to live intentionally without going broke in the process.

If it's not in the budget, you can't get the new iPhone. If it's not in the budget, you can't go out to eat. If it's not in the budget, you'll have to wait. I know this is difficult since we live in an "on-demand" society. But there's nothing wrong with waiting for something you want until you have the money for it. Practicing delayed gratification does two things:

1. It stops you from getting into debt

2. It will make sure that you really want this item.

How many times have we bought something, had to pay it back, and in a month or two, never used it again? Delayed gratification helps to stop both problems at the same time. If you want something, you can save your hard-earned money for a month or two and then get it.

There's a term that's becoming more popular: the *hedonic treadmill*. The hedonic treadmill is the tendency of a person to remain at a relatively stable level of happiness despite a change in fortune or the achievement of major goals.

In other words, we buy something because we really, really want it. We think it's cool. We think that it's going to make us feel happy, and it does at first. But after a short time, it doesn't really matter to us anymore. We don't give it a priority in our life. An example of this is with kids and their toys. How often has your kid whined and begged for a certain toy only to have it buried in their toy chest a few days or weeks after?

We, as adults, experience the hedonic treadmill too. We want that new iPhone because we think it will make us feel cool or make our friends jealous, so we buy it, even though our old phone still works. Then after a few days, we don't even think about it, and we're onto the next thing. Our intention with our purchase is to make us happier. The outcome of this purchase doesn't live up to the expectation. Welcome to the hedonic treadmill.

The only way to solve this dilemma is to get off the treadmill and live intentionally with your money. Living intentionally means prioritizing the things you spend your money on. Living and not just possessing. Do you want a house full of stuff you don't care about, or do you want to live in a house full of stuff you love and use daily?

Are you buying this item because you need it or want it? Are you buying it to keep up with your friends or coworkers? If you're trying to keep up with the imaginary Joneses, let me tell you something: it won't make you happy. All it will do is create a money nightmare that will cause you to spend your time working at a job you hate so you can pay the debt these items have caused you to be in.

In today's society, peer pressure has shifted from doing certain things to buying certain things. What peer pressure has done is create an America that's not free anymore but is shackled in consumer debt, which we already explored in Chapter 3.

So the question is: How are you going to live your life? Are you going to spend your resources on living your life to its fullest, the way you want to live it? Or will you live your life for others, doing things and spending money to impress others?

True freedom is living our lives doing what we want to do, when we want to do it, and with whom we want to do it! True freedom comes with maturity and intention and can only be lived if we let go of the peer pressure's grip it has on us. That's living with intention.

Attitude

"For success, attitude is equally as important as ability."-Walter Scott

Our attitudes toward life, in general, can have a humongous effect on the outcomes we experience on a daily basis. Some of us believe the glass is half empty, so why bother? It will all be gone soon enough. Others believe that the glass is half full and that it's our responsibility and privilege to go out and fill up the rest ourselves.

I like to believe that the glass is half full and that I want to see how full I can make it. I'm intentionally trying to fill up my glass. I fill it with experiences. I fill it with people I love and who are important to me. I fill it by writing and learning new concepts. I fill it with adventure. I fill it with creativity. I'm always looking for ways and things that will help to fill up my glass.

It's a good metaphor for attitude. According to Dictionary.com, *attitude* means "A settled way of thinking or feeling about someone or something, typically one that is reflected in a person's behavior."

The way we think about something, our belief systems, causes us to behave in a certain way resulting in habit formation. We learn what to place value on by our environment and our experience. This, of course, can change over our lifetime. But when it's all said and done, we must find our *why* if we're to live intentionally. This all boils down to our perception of things, how we look at life in general, and our overall attitude toward it.

Attitude is made up of thoughts, feelings, and behaviors about something. If we spend all of our money because we think that other people are judging us, then our attitude will cause us to always be upgrading our lives to keep up with others' opinions. If we spend all of our time working on things that aren't essential to our success, then we will always be out of time to spend on the things that will make us happy.

Tony Robbins says, "Stop majoring in minor things." When we allow others to use up our resources first, we normally won't have any leftovers to spend the way we want. That's why living with intention is critical to living the life we deserve and desire.

If we're always complaining and blaming others for our problems, that's having the attitude that we aren't in control of our lives, thoughts, and actions. This is simply the wrong attitude. We are in *control* of our attitude and how we react to other people and events that we interact with.

If we live with the attitude of being in the present, controlling what we can, and letting the rest go, we can slow things down and make the most of each moment. If we feel grateful for all of the blessings in our lives, we can't concurrently feel negative about the world and how unfair it's treating us. A positive attitude attracts other positive things.

Of course, bad things will happen to us. We'll lose our jobs. We'll injure ourselves. Something will break that will cost time and money to fix. Our overall attitude toward life will help us get through these difficult situations. During a difficult time in American history when he was taking office, Abraham Lincoln said, "This too shall pass."

If we take a look at the overall picture of our lives, we will find our attitude front and center of the results we're getting. If we believe that nothing will ever work out, we won't take the actions necessary for them to work out. If we believe nothing matters, we won't take the necessary actions to make them matter. If we think it, we feel it, and move our lives in that direction.

There are so many victims in the world. Some of them don't have the freedom we here in the United States have to make our lives better. To live intentionally. There doesn't seem to be an excuse for why we live in the most opportunity-driven nation in society. Yet, 59 million people or 19% of the population, are on welfare. Why so many?

It starts with their attitudes about their lives and opportunities to live the way they want. Most of these people are second and third-generation welfare recipients. They are taught to believe that they can't be important in their society. They believe that there's nothing for society to provide for them, so they don't take the necessary action to make something worthwhile happen in their life. They don't participate in the educational system. They turn to crime and drug abuse and make their situations worse. Some people do make it out of the system and build a wonderful life. But it all starts with building an attitude of *I can* instead of *I can't*. That simple change can affect everything and everyone around them and change the generations of their family forever.

Living with intention. Knowing what's important and saying no to the rest. Filling your mind and your heart with love and hope for a better tomorrow. Working toward your goals and not allowing obstacles to get in the way of living your fullest life. That's what living with intention is about. Not allowing things, commitments, social pressures, or obligations to stand in the way of living your purpose and reaching your potential. Having the freedom to choose how you live your life. Choosing what to do and who to spend it with is the ultimate luxury anyone with a good attitude can encapsulate.

The Roman Emperor Marcus Aurelius said, "Memento Mori. You could leave life right now. Let that determine what you do, say, and think." We will all die, and we don't know when this will be. If that doesn't create a sense of urgency to live with intention, I don't know what else could. If we knew the exact day, hour, and minute we would die, we might plan our lives differently. But we don't. We don't know when we will get sick. When our heart will stop beating. Or if we will be involved in an accident that will cease our bodily functions. We don't know when that will be.

Will you be satisfied that you lived your best life if you die tomorrow? If you die tomorrow, will you accept that you tried your hardest, were a good person, and left your mark on the world the best you knew how?

This is definitely something to think about. Live with intention. Spend your precious resources the way you want. Live with freedom to enjoy your life doing what you want, when you want, and with who you want. We all have this freedom of choice. Yes, we will occasionally do things we don't necessarily want to do. Yes, we will waste our resources in a way that doesn't serve us. But not every day. Not in every way.

We must *live* our lives. This is the only life we've got, as far as we know. 20 years, 50 years, or 100 years isn't a lot of time when you look at the big picture. Human beings have been around for over two million years. Earth itself is estimated to be over four billion years old. So your lifespan is a tiny grain of dust in the hourglass of time. How we use this tiny grain makes all the difference to us, our family, and mankind as a whole.

How will we contribute? How will we make things better, faster, easier, or cheaper for others? What will we leave for our families? Wisdom? Money? A method for living with intention? Yes, I think about these things all of the time. I think this is what one does when one turns 40. I think this is what your "midlife crisis" entails. Although I'm almost 50, I still think about these things daily.

Memento mori. We don't have to dwell on death, but we should embrace life and live it the way we want. If we want to travel, we should do it. If we want to move, we should do it. If we want to have a family, we should do it. If we want to find a new job or return to school, we should do it. Let urgency be alive within your spirit and your will to get things done and make a change for the better.

It all boils down to our attitudes. If we think about it, we can do it. If we're positive and put in the effort, anything is possible. In Neville Goddard's *Feeling is the Secret*, he writes, "Be careful of your moods and feelings, for there is an unbroken connection between your feelings and your visible world. All you can possibly need or desire is already yours. You need no helper to give it to you; it is yours now."

Playing victim or having a negative belief about something will not help the situation. We will live the way we feel. It is up to us to go into every situation with positive energy, be willing to give it our best and be eager to contribute our talents to the world. That's the attitude of a person living with intention!

Focus

"Concentrate all your thoughts upon the work at hand. The sun's rays do not burn until brought to a focus."- Alexander Graham Bell

Living with intention narrows your focus on living your life the way you want. That takes awareness of your past, where you're currently, and where you want to go. It also means that you must focus on what that dream life entails and get rid of the distractions you will face that steer you away from it.

Many racehorse trainers believe blinders keep horses focused on what is in front of them, encouraging them to pay attention to the race rather than to distractions such as crowds and other horses. Additionally, driving horses commonly wear blinders to keep them from being distracted or spooked, especially on crowded city streets.

What blinders can you enforce in your life to keep your focus and attention on living intentionally? Maybe that's a written budget that maps out your spending and saving intentions. Maybe that's using Google calendar to map out times during the day that you want to accomplish a workout, training, or even reading. Maybe that's meal prepping for the week so that your meals are already portioned and available to you when you're hungry.

Living intentionally takes focused attention and awareness of the steps needed to live the way you desire.

It's the *how* of the goal-achieving process. You may not know every step you need to take to create the life you want to live. But knowing the general habits and behaviors successful people take to live the way you want is a start in the right direction. And that's all that matters. It's the daily grind that creates weeks, months, and years that compound and build on themselves.

Martha Beck wrote, "How you do anything is how you do everything." If you're sweeping the floor, are you sweeping it to the best of your ability? Are you focused on getting all the dirt and debris off the floor or lazily sweeping without intention? We can all do things without clear intentions. Sometimes we can find ourselves just going through the motions. Not really focusing on what we're doing and why we're doing it. To live intentionally, we must focus on our purpose and why we're doing and living the way we are.

Are we doing our best? Are we being intentional with our resources, or are we just acting out of habit or convenience? Sometimes we will follow the herd. But to live intentionally, we must break free from the herd and be true to ourselves and our desires for a well-lived life. That will mean different things to different people. And that's wonderful!

That's what makes the people and relationships we build with them so wonderful. It's great to meet people that live differently from us. That's how we learn and grow. That's how we become aware of our differences, and it helps us focus on the things we want for our lives. If your neighbor does something that you would like to do, change your actions. Change your focus. Change them, and you, too, can do what your neighbor does.

But it starts with focus. We must put on the blinders and focus our resources and attention on what we want to get out of our lives. We must avoid and discard the distractions that will try their best to derail our efforts. All of us can be, do, or have whatever we want. But it all starts with focusing all our resources on that end goal. It's lasering in our efforts toward that end focal point. Like a laser beaming all of its energy on one small area, we can do the same with our attention. Our focus. Our effort.

To live intentionally means to focus. It means using our resources most effectively and efficiently to close the gap between where we are and where we want to go. Focus your attention on your resources, become aware of what areas you're deficient in, and create opportunities to build on those deficiencies until you are proficient in those areas. Focus.

Chapter 8

People

"You can't change the people around you,
but you *can* change the people around
you."-Joshua Fields Millburn

In other words, you can't change how other people
think, act, or feel, but you can surround yourself with
people that support you and your mission in life. As we
circumvent our way on our life journey, the first people we
surround ourselves with are our family and friends. One
thing that's true for all is that we can't choose our family.
Cells join from our parents and create us. We can't control
this; it is out of our control.

We then go to school and participate in activities
and rituals important to our communities and families.
But when we're adults, we somehow have the freedom of
choice that was never privy to us growing up.

We can choose what we do with our lives. We can
choose what career we have. We can choose who we fall in

love with. We can choose where to live, what to eat for dinner, and what house we buy. We have the freedom to choose all of it or none of it. If we want this, then we must do this. If we don't want that, we don't do that. It's all about choice. Throughout this book, we're diving into these choices that we can make or don't want to make. A big component of our choices comes down to the people we surround ourselves with.

Who are they, and what makes them tick?

Family

"Families are like branches on a tree. They grow in different directions yet they come from the same roots."– Unknown

---

Some of us are lucky to have great families. Some of us are not. A family doesn't necessarily need to be defined by genetic code. It can be a choice. As adults, friends in our inner circle are often closer to us and more important to us than our blood relatives. The people who raise us have a direct influence over our beliefs and thoughts initially. They help to mold us as young children. We see how our families react and respond to different circumstances. We see what they love. We see and experience what they hate. These ideas can directly influence how we see the world and our role in it.

The great thing about family is they can shortcut our learning curve when it comes to success. Of course, our family needs to *have* success for us to benefit from their knowledge. Experience and knowledge can go hand in hand when it comes to absorbing information from our family. How were we brought up? What beliefs were we led to trust? How do they answer questions about wealth, relationships, and health?

Are they wealthy? If so, we can learn what to do and not do in our careers to build wealth. Do they invest? How? What vehicles do they use to build their wealth? Do they own their own businesses? Are they consultants? Do they travel? Do they work for someone else? What industry are they in? Is there a future in that industry for the next generation? Do they own real estate? Why type? Where? What other methods of wealth creation are they involved in? Do they invest in stocks? What kind? When do they buy or sell?

Are they healthy? What do they believe in concerning their diet? What about exercise? Do they run? Do they bike? Are they still active in sports? What about their diet? How do they eat? Are they vegetarian? Do they take supplements? Which ones? Do they go to the doctor regularly to monitor their vital signs and blood components?

What about relationships? Are they still married to their spouse? Are they divorced? Do they value family? Do they value building their networks inside and outside their work? Are they religious? Do they belong to a religious sect? Do they believe in charity? How do they give back?

Are they political? Do they vote often? What party do they belong to? Do they help with political events? Do they support the people in office or the party they belong to?

Many of our beliefs and early experiences come directly from our families. If our families are not successful, our beliefs and values will be completely different than if we come from success. Success always builds on itself because the success code has been cracked, and wealthy families teach their children how to keep and multiply the wealth that the family has built. They always say that making the first million dollars is the hardest part. After that, it snowballs and becomes easier and easier to grow.

The great thing about our families is that we can love them, but we can also not allow them to control our thoughts once we become adults. That doesn't mean we're not close to them or need to keep them away. But it can mean that we won't allow them to influence our beliefs and actions if they haven't demonstrated that their thoughts and actions align with our own.

As adults, we can determine what our lives will look like and either our families can help get us to the finish line or hinder our progress. Either way, we need to recognize who we let into our lives and inner circles and not trust the opinions of people. Some that may be very close to us, if they won't help us get to the place in our lives that we wish to go[AS2] . It's as simple as that.

We need to recognize what steps are necessary to reach our goals, whether financially, spiritually, or in our health. I don't take any advice from anyone who hasn't hit the goal I want to achieve. If they're obese and unhealthy, I wouldn't ask them for recipes or advice on anything that has to do with my body. If they're broke, don't invest, and spend more than they earn, I won't ask them how to become wealthy. They have no clue and can't teach me anything! If I'm trying to become a better person and want to grow and contribute my talents to the world, I definitely wouldn't ask the advice of someone who has no social connections and spouts negativity in every conversation they have. They can't lead me down the right path.

Creating the right relationships with people that can create the right environment that leads me to my goals in my life is the only thing I should be concerned with. And it's okay if you outgrow your group. That means you're accomplishing your goals. That means you're growing and getting better. That means you're succeeding. So if this is you, continue looking for other people that can help you take your life to the next step. Whether that's financially, spiritually, or with your health. Keep growing. Keep improving. Remember, all you have is time. Do the most you can with the time you have. Concentrate your thoughts and actions on success. Spend your time wisely with people that have your best interests at heart. Spend time with people that are already successful and are now spending their time helping you through your journey as mentors. Everyone needs mentors in their lives to help them leapfrog to their next goal. But the right mentors at the right time are required to find success. The wrong mentor at the wrong time may lead you down the wrong alley and can hinder your success rather than guarantee it.

The Norms/Cliches

> "If you are always trying to be normal, you will never know how amazing you can be."– Maya Angelou

Society can produce average people. Average thoughts and average actions that get average results. If you don't want to be average, stay away from the norms or cliches of society. Never, never go with the crowd. That doesn't mean they are completely wrong, but they may have left out some important details needed to get you to your goals. They may have cut corners, not followed the correct steps, or stopped short of reaching success because they never believed they could do it in the first place. Cliches and norms can kill your success. Awareness of what the average people do with their lives can help you not become one of them.

Most people are told to mind their own business. Don't create attention. Don't talk to strangers. Grant Cardone says, "Talk to strangers because strangers have everything you want." And for the most part, this is true. How will you expand your network of clients if you don't meet new people? How will you know if the new person you meet could be the love of your life or your next business partner? Unless you put yourself out into the world and take a chance, you'll never get anywhere new. Of course, I'm not telling you to go talk to people in shady neighborhoods at midnight, but meeting new people is essential to improving your life.

What about the saying, "Don't create attention?" To market yourself, you need to create attention. How will people ever know that you and your products and services are available if you don't cause attention? What if you are interested in that person at work or sitting at the bar? If you don't bring attention to yourself and your wants, how will they ever know you're interested in them? Life and success are all about attention. Who knows you is more important than who you know. If people know you, your moral character, talents, and success, they will want to be around you more. They will want to do business with you. They may even want an intimate relationship with you. All because they know who you are.

What about the saying, "Read between the lines." Words can matter, but actions can verify the real truth behind the words. It's okay to have a verbal agreement with someone, but to cover your bases and protect yourself, your money, and your mind, back it up with something in writing.

This saying could also mean that something that is said or meant is hidden from the words. Maybe you get in a fight with your loved one, and they say you did something against them on purpose. Do they really mean that? Or do they mean they really want your support on this idea or thing they're attempting to do, but you're blocking their progress? Maybe you're doing it on purpose, or maybe you're doing it subconsciously because you truly don't agree with them. That doesn't mean that you disagree with them all the time, maybe on this particular subject.

What about when your child yells at you because you moved their favorite hat? Are they really yelling at you because you moved their favorite hat to clean? Or is it because they're tired and frustrated because they didn't sleep a lot the night before and don't want to put in the effort to look for their favorite hat, so they take their frustration out on you.

A useful term in sales is the hidden objective. Maybe you're trying to sell someone your product, and they tell you that they need to talk to their spouse about it. Is that their true objective or just an excuse to not buy your product? Maybe your product doesn't solve their problem, wants, or need, and they're too polite or afraid to tell you the truth. Unless you ask questions and do more fact-finding on the true reason they don't want to buy from you, you'll never get a sale because most people don't want to be sold to. They want to control and be in charge.

What about the saying, "It's a big bad world out there; better make sure you stay close to home, so you're safe." According to Northamerican.com, 72% of people live near the city where they grew up. 72%. There are almost 8 billion people on planet Earth. If you live where you grew up, you may have only met a few hundred people in your life, not a few thousand.

How will you expand your thinking, beliefs, network, and material wealth if you stay in the same place your whole life? Today, we have the internet, which can connect us to half of the planet that has access to it. So this can open up bridges to new friends and colleagues we've never had access to. But being in the small-town frame of mind cannot help anyone expand their ideas, communication, culture, or choices. It's impossible when the quotient of possibilities is so small. In truth, the possibilities of anything are infinite, and we need to make sure we expand on those possibilities.

What about the saying, "Kiss and make up?" This can help your relationships, but can it save your spiritual growth? If you're always fighting with your lover and there's no compromise to the situation, will you continue to be stuck in the same routine day after day? At some point, we all need to expand and grow; to do that, we need the freedom to move on.

If a client is always fighting with you about your products or their bill, is it worth pursuing future business from them? Or is it easier to deal with your other 100 clients who never give you a hassle and are always willing to listen to your pitches? If your environment and peer group have negative beliefs about advancement and success, will this allow you to expand or contract?

Sometimes changes need to be made to take our lives to the next step. This doesn't mean that love and forgiveness aren't in order. This doesn't mean that you don't get your way every time that you disappear. This means that we all must draw a line in the sand, decide when enough is enough, and move on to another space in life.

What about opposites attract? This can be a good thing in business if the things you're opposite about with your partner complement each other. If you're good at marketing and your partner has a product to sell, this is a match made in heaven.

If your lover is an ambitious, energetic person, and you want to stay in the same place you've always been, how would this ever work out? You'll always be complaining that they're not spending enough time with you, and they'll always be complaining that you're holding them back from their dreams. It won't work. Opposites only work out if they complement each other and can add to each other's outcomes.

What about the saying, "Don't cry over spilled milk?" We can't change the fact that something has happened, so why cry or worry over it? Take situations for just that. Situations. When it's over, it's in the past, and there's nothing we can do to change it.

But we can change the present. We can make different decisions in our lives today. We can do things differently. We can take action. We can hang out with different people. We can change our beliefs and attitudes. We can set goals. We can network. We can take responsibility for our lives and choices.

What about the saying, "Haste makes waste."
Think about the numerous times you bought something
cheap because you didn't want to spend a lot of money on
the item only to have it break a few days or weeks later. If
you had researched, taken your time, and bought a better
brand of item, you could still be using it today. Nowadays,
there are many ways to research a decision.

We can use the internet to research anything from
careers, colleges, loan rates, apparel, appliances, and even
houses. It's always better to take our time to thoroughly
investigate the pros and cons of a purchase or major
decision that affects our life rather than make a quick
decision that could be burdensome.

What about the saying, "Time heals all wounds."
When we get angry about something, we tend to react
with emotion instead of responding with logic. Do you
even need to express your opinion if something happens
to you? If someone cuts you off in traffic, do you need to
retaliate and flip them the bird? Maybe they have an
emergency to get to and drive a little crazy. You don't
know their circumstances.

Again, the circumstances are out of your control.
But what is in control is how you react to the situation.
Maybe you're in an argument with your lover. Is the

argument really that important? Or can you compromise or even give in so you can move on with your relationship? Many of the things that fill our days are not even in our memory banks, days, weeks, months, and even years later. Do you remember why you were fighting with your brother last year? Do you remember getting angry with your boss over that project last week? If you allow time to come between the argument and the solution, most of the negative emotions will dissipate into the ether, and the logical solution can evolve.

What goes around comes around. This is The Law of Cause and Effect and karma. Whatever you do will have consequences. Whatever you reap, you will sow. If you're negative, you'll live a negative life. Opportunities will forgo your path, and the Universe will reward its bounty to other people. If you eat fast food every day, your health will start suffering. If you spend all of your money on stupid stuff, you will lack financial security and freedom. If you are violent, you will never have love in your life. What you put out into the Universe will come back into your life like a boomerang.

What about the saying, "When life gives you lemons, make lemonade." I love this quote. Not everything you plan will turn out the way you want it to.

Projects. Situations. Plans. Relationships. Sometimes you need to pivot. Sometimes you need to creatively find the not-so-obvious solution to the problem. Sometimes you're forced into a difficult situation. Maybe you need help with something you thought you could do alone. No matter what happens, know there's a solution to any problem.

Choice

"No matter what the situation, remind yourself, I Have a Choice." –Deepak Chopra

---

The main thing to know in this chapter is that we are given the choice of free will. Whether we live in the United States or Ghana, we have the choice to think the way we want to think. Now some countries restrict the actions that can be taken by individual citizens. But in all instances, governments and institutions cannot control our thoughts and beliefs.

Having said that, living in the United States has given us a chance to act on our thoughts and beliefs. We have the Constitutional right to be free and pursue our happiness, despite what government regulations restrict. If we live in a bad neighborhood, we have the choice to change it. If we find ourselves overweight and unhealthy, we have the choice to change it. If we find ourselves hating our jobs, we have the choice to change them. If we aren't in a relationship that serves us, we have the choice to change it.

No matter how old we are, where we come from, or what we want to change, we have the right to choose something different for our lives.

Isn't that the most freeing thing you've ever heard? I'm a woman. If I lived in another country, I might not have the same rights I have here in America. I can choose anything I want in my life. My friends. My job. My dreams. My husband. My network. My health. I feel so blessed and grateful that my ancestors gave me the freedom of choice.

The question is, what am I going to do with it? The same question is posed to you. What are you going to do with your freedom to choose? Choose where you want to live. Choose what type of partner you want in your life. Choose what business you own or work in. Choose your financial life. Choose your health status. There are thousands and thousands of choices you will face throughout your life. The great thing about all of these choices is that if one choice doesn't serve you anymore, you can simply choose something else.

It's that simple. It doesn't matter if it will hurt someone's feelings. It doesn't matter if it goes against other people's wants. What matters is what *you* want. What matters is what your goals for your life are. And throughout your life, you'll find that some goals will change. That's what is fun and interesting about life if you decide to take control of it and make choices according to your happiness and fulfillment measurements.

Any and all choices that we make come with consequences. If we say yes to something, we are equally saying no to something else. If we buy this thing, we are giving up a choice to buy something else at the same time because our money, as well as our time and energy, are finite. There is only so much time, energy, and money to go around. We must deliberate extensively over our choices and try to make the correct ones out of the gate so that our finite resources aren't wasted.

Yes, we can always change our choices and choose something else, but in the long run, we must take our freedom of choice very seriously. If we choose the wrong path or thing or person to bring into our lives, we can set ourselves up for failure. Choices can be complicated.

Choices can take time to make. Choices can be difficult to handle. But I would rather have the freedom to choose something difficult to handle or complicated than have someone else choose that thing for me.

That doesn't mean that choice can't be linked with cooperation or compromise because it can be. We all must make compromises and even sacrifices for our choices. Sometimes there's not a clear choice to make that helps everyone win. Sometimes we must choose to take one step backward to jump two steps forward.

Sometimes we must choose to wait for our gratification because waiting to decide to buy something, marry someone, or make a move in our career can mean that we're ready for it and can handle it at a later time when the situation warrants itself.

Sometimes the freedom of choice can be overwhelming when you know that the world is your oyster and you have the freedom to do anything you want. But you can easily decrease your choice anxiety by asking yourself, " Is the choice I'm making moving me toward or further away from my immediate goal?"

If choosing to buy a new car this week prohibits you from saving at least 30% of your income to invest in retirement opportunities, you wouldn't make that choice. You would wait. If eating that Snickers bar would prohibit you from losing the ten pounds you've been working toward for the past two months, you wouldn't make that choice. If your partner wanted to change product lines that aren't as profitable or accessible as those your company currently sells, you wouldn't agree to make that change.

Choices can either help or hinder our life's purpose. They can either help us progress toward our goals or pull us back and keep us stuck in our current spot. The people we surround ourselves with and take advice from directly influence our choices. So remember to surround yourself with people moving toward the goals you want to obtain. Make sure you take advice from people already walking the walk and talking the talk. Don't associate with people that can either halt your goal achievement or even damage the progress that you've already made. That doesn't mean you can't love them or spend time with them; you can't model your life and your choices after theirs.

Jim Rohn said, "Your life is equivalent to the five people that you associate the most with." This can mean income. This can mean relationships. This can mean their general attitude toward life. If they are negative in all of their conversations, could that possibly rub off on you? If they cheat or talk negatively about their marriage, can that directly influence you and your actions? If they are caught up in comparison and keeping up with the latest fashions and trends, do you think you'll feel pressure from them to do the same thing? Of course! This is why choosing people in your inner circle is vitally important to your future success.

Children

"Old men can make war, but it is children who will make history."- Ray Merritt

---

Children are all a blessing. As parents, we have the privilege of reliving our childhood- our likes and hates as well as our previous experiences through our children. But how important do we take this responsibility? The average age in the US to have children is 26.3 years, according to CDC.gov. This is an increase from 24.9 years old in 2000. As the new generations work through the culture, it's agreed that working on building a career, especially for women, is important. Long hours, moving up the corporate ladder, and building networks in our early 20s are part of the norm. Focusing on long-term relationships and children seems to take the back burner.

And I think this is okay. I wanted to build my own practice and didn't want to settle down with a family until I had my ducks all in a row financially and maturaley[AS3] . For anyone in their 30s, think back to those early 20s when you had little responsibility. Do you think you were mature enough to handle everything you can handle now? Of course not. What about those of you in your 40s? Think of all the things you do today, and do well compared to how you were living five, ten, or even twenty years ago.

The course of our lives changes as we age. Our priorities change. The people we let into our professional networks and our personal tribes change over time. I know I have separated from the toxic relationships I have had in my past. These people didn't contribute to my life, and deciding to separate from them and not hold counsel to their advice was one of the best things I could have done.

The same thing goes for toxic ideas and beliefs. As we age and mature, we gain experiences that we can draw from. Was my belief that I could get into shape and stay in shape correct? Was my theory that the average man can't get ahead and build wealth really true? What about my thoughts on building and raising a family with someone I love?

When I first started practicing dentistry, I was all in. I took every continuing education course there was on the planet. I learned everything I could about marketing and business management. I got to the office early and stayed late. I worked at multiple offices while I started my practice and absorbed as much information from the other dentists and team members as possible. In my mind, there was no room for children in that life. It was all about my practice. I had to think that way because I had tremendous debt from school and started my own practice. I had loans up to my eyeballs. One equipment loan, I remember, was at 11% interest! Wow! I knew I had to hustle to make things work. And I did.

Then I met my husband, spent a lot of time with his family, and caught the baby bug. This led us down the path of starting our own family. I was almost 38 when I had my son. In retrospect, I am so glad that I waited. First of all, I had paid off my debt which put us on the path to financial security. Second, I had built up the practice, so it was at a comfortable level and was on cruise control. I knew I could devote my time and energy toward my son and husband compared to only my business.

Most people in their 20s are still focused on themselves, which they should be. They need at least ten years to figure out what path they want to lead in life. Once in their 30s, most people are settled in their career field and can focus their resources on other pursuits, like intimate relationships and family. They have time. They have money. They also have the maturity level to give their love to someone other than themselves.

They have the experience and patience to teach their children what they truly need to know. They have discipline. They can provide enriching experiences. They focus on making sure their children have a better life than they themselves may have had.

In my book, *The Habit Formula- Kids' Edition*, I write extensively on the importance of building good habits in your children. But what if we don't have good habits? How can we teach our children about building wealth when we don't have good money habits? A 2014 study by The National Bureau of Economic Research found that parents on welfare have children that also end up on welfare. Why is that? It's because the parents surround the children with a culture of welfare acceptance. The same is true for ultra-wealthy families. The ultra-wealthy families bring their children into a wealthy mindset and teach them money and career habits that steer them away from lack and toward abundance.

This doesn't necessarily mean that what parents teach children are the children's end results, but they can be. This is why it is very important to ensure you're ready and mature enough to bring children into this world. With rising social and economic tension around the world, we need to make sure we have security and safety in our lives before we expand our responsibilities toward someone else. This can include having secure careers, financial means to properly care for our families, time to spend with them, and cultural habits we want to pass on to them. So a good rule of thumb: care about *yourself* and become the person you want to become *before* you create another person.

Intimate Relationships

"Those that have never known the deep
intimacy and the intense companionship
of happy mutual love have missed the best
thing that life has to give."- Bertrand
Russell

Everyone has found love at some point in their lives. How deep and intimate that love becomes depends on the willingness of both partners to share and grow their lives together. It takes a lot of work to create an intimate relationship that lasts. Yet, it is an essential part of our human experience.

A 2018 study done in the *Journal of Health Psychology* found a 20% drop in early death among people that were in happy long-term relationships. This study also linked trimmer waistlines and healthier cardiovascular function in people that were in happy long-term relationships.

People that live together become habits themselves. I've been married for almost 15 years. My husband knows what role he plays. He fixes stuff, is messy and messes the house up, and is in charge of killing large insects in the house. He knows what he's supposed to do and does them automatically. My role is to clean up his messes, invest our money wisely, and plan fun trips and events. I know what I'm supposed to do, and I do them automatically. These are habitual habits for him and me, and neither one of us has to redefine our roles in our relationship every day.

That's what an intimate relationship can do for you. It can help you define your role in your home. It can help you find peace and security inside yourself and your abilities. I don't have to be interesting to the rest of the world; I only have to be interesting to one person. And that is so freeing and satisfying. That doesn't mean that I'm supposed to get fat and lazy. That means I can grow and improve myself. It also means that he can still love the growth and improvements I create for myself.

Is it easier to finish a project yourself or with a team helping you? Of course, with a team helping you. What about saving and investing for financial independence? Is it easier to do it all by yourself or with someone pitching in? Of course, it's easier to act as a team to become debt free and build wealth with a combined effort. It's always easier to build something with a team as long as the team is fully on board with the plans you want to carry out.

Intimate relationships are a difficult subject to tackle. But one thing to know is that you must find common ground with your partner if you're going to build a life together. This means compromise, planning, and working together on your common goals. This means trusting that your partner has your best interest at heart.

Having sex with someone is a wonderful way of spending some time. Yes, it feels good, and the instant satisfaction you feel from your hormone rush is quite delightful. But building a life with someone you have nothing in common with except sexual chemistry is prone to disaster. Values, beliefs, children, and living as a couple rise above all else.

If you're constantly stressed or always walking on eggshells around your partner, you should move on to another person. Women are especially vulnerable to physical and mental abuse. Depending on their environment growing up, women can tend to become involved with men who act similarly to their fathers or men they grew up with. This can be good or bad depending on abuse issues that may come up.

Happiness always starts within, but having a partner that agrees with your values and goals can make life easy and fun. It's always good to focus on yourself before involving someone else in your life journey. Are there things you want to improve? If you're without excess baggage, someone will want to join your life journey with you. If you bring too much baggage to the journey, others will notice and keep passing you by. Find confidence and success within your own life and share it with the world. People will notice and be attracted to you. Choose your partner wisely, and if it doesn't work out, there's always someone out there that's a better match.

Sales

"It's no longer about interrupting, pitching and closing. It is about listening, diagnosing and prescribing." – Mark Roberge

---

Let's face it. Everyone is in sales. Even if you're a mechanic, dishwasher, or dentist. We're all in it to help others with the products and services that we represent. Dictionary.com defines *sales* as "the exchange of a commodity for money; the action of selling something." But we're going to talk not only about selling something for an exchange of money but also about selling something for abstract things that have little to do with money. This could be time, satisfaction, cause and effect, etc.

If someone was hurt and you were the only one who could help them, would you? Of course! As humans, we have the instinct to help each other in times of need. Even though the other person doesn't *pay* you with money, they often *pay* you with other things like gratitude, reciprocation of help in the future, or even homemade gifts. This can still be considered a sale. You've exchanged something useful with another person. Rabbi Daniel Lapin, who wrote *Thou Shall Prosper,* says, "Delight in helping others. It's the best advice you will ever get."

Many things in life come with an exchange fee. For thousands of years, humans have been exchanging ideas, products, and services to solve problems we all face. Physical problems. Spiritual problems. Mental and emotional problems. Since the dawn of recorded history, humans have written and spoken of stories to one another about lessons that others have learned to help future generations springboard from those lessons. As the saying goes, "History often repeats itself."

This is because sometimes those history lessons are hidden in divisive topics like religion, psychology, and philosophy. Most people aren't educated in these areas; thus, the lessons learned from the past get lost with each generation that follows. This can result in treachery, death, and pain that could be avoided simply by learning the lessons of the past.

So what does this have to do with sales? Learning how to think, act, and behave professionally and personally can help you become a successful employee or business owner. It's learning the lessons of those who preceded you that can help you understand people and what they want. In his book, *Sell or Be Sold*, Grant Cardone writes, "A person's ability to persuade another is the only thing that will ultimately ensure a position in the marketplace."

According to Pew Research, the average American reads twelve books per year. That's a book a month. The *Published to Death* blog cited that the most popular genre of books read in this country is mystery, thriller, and crime. Yes, you could learn a lot about the evil psychotic thoughts and actions of mankind in this type of genre. But these types of books won't ultimately help you add to your network of clients, reach your career goals, or make you more money. How can you learn to communicate with others and figure out what they want from you if your mind is filled with fiction nonsense?

Communication is the cornerstone of not only sales but also understanding. If you don't understand what people want, there's no way to help them. In *The Communication Parable*, SHE struggles with getting her team to communicate in the same way, understand what needs to be done to complete their projects, and turn that communication into actionable steps. In the end, SHE finds out that communication can never be mastered. Both parties need to make sure they communicate so that the other person understands what they're saying. The easiest way to communicate with someone is to ask a question and keep asking it differently until an answer is spoken. If we fail to communicate, we fail to understand, and we fail to help.

Whether you're directly in sales or not, communicating with someone starts with finding common ground. There's something in common that two people can find. It could be personal. It could be professional. It could be cultural. All that's needed is one thing in common that can help build a solid communication foundation.

If you're trying to ask your boss for a promotion, an easy way toward rejection is to force a one-way communication on them. This one-way communication could include why you deserve a raise, comparison with others, or using a certain timeframe. There's no room for your boss to meet you on the common ground because the foundation you're building is solely all about *you* and your wants and needs.

Instead, a better way to communicate this is to ask for more responsibility in your job. Ask what your boss and the company need and fill that void. You may not receive a monetary reward in the beginning of this new venture. But at some point, you will be offered either a different position with more pay or a newly created one with more pay. Because you chose to help first and not ask for a reward for previous acts, you convince your boss you deserve to make more money and share your ideas for the overall good of the company's mission.

Network

Your network is your net worth."– Tim Sanders

"Contacts equal contracts." This small quote has a hugely important lesson in it. Without other people, you can't succeed. To be successful in life, you must develop relationships. The "r" in contracts stands for relationships. That's the difference between contacts and contracts. It's the "r" or relationships that are missing.

This goes for a business owner or a sports team. If no other people are involved in their project, then they have no project. If you just opened a pizza shop, how will you pay your rent, pay your employees, and make a living if you don't have customers consuming your food? If you have a team, but you're the only one on it, how will you win against a team with ten people? It just won't work without other people. That's where relationships come into play. We need other people. We need customers. We need team members. We need technology. We need a network.

How do you talk to someone if you don't know them? We all need to create rapport with that person. According to Dictionary.com, rapport means "a close and harmonious relationship in which the people or groups concerned understand each other's feelings or ideas and communicate well." Rapport is very easy to create, and it's done by asking questions. Find out what the other person likes. Find out what their problem is. Find out some opinions of the other person. Once you do some fact-finding, you can create rapport with that person by finding commonalities that you share.

What is the easiest way to be a good conversationalist? In their blog, *Fast Company* explained six habits of being a better conversationalist. Listening to the other person more than talking to them is the number one best way to converse. Being interested in what they say and feeding off them is the easiest way to converse with someone you don't know. What is the one person people love talking about the most? That's right- themselves. So if you're striking up a conversation with someone, be interested in them and what topics they want to talk about.

This can also work in business negotiations. If you're cold calling a person you don't know, you can first ask them questions about their businesses and find out their problems. Then you can figure out whether your products and services can properly solve their problems. You can accomplish this by listening and talking about them instead of yourself first.

Another way to converse easily is to admit when you don't know something. No one likes a *know-it-all*. I have met these kinds of people, and I don't particularly care to hang out with them. They always want to have better stories than you. They always want to be right. They always have opinions about *everything*. Who wants to talk with someone like that?

To be good conversationalists, we must learn when to interject our own opinions or experiences and when not. Will our interjections matter or improve the way this conversation is going? If not, let it go. Keep quiet and allow the conversation to die on its own. I do this a lot with people that have vast differences in opinion. I don't need to be right about everything, and if they say something that I don't agree with, I mostly stay quiet and try to change the subject.

To build rapport with someone, finding activities, hobbies, or interests that are similar are also easy ways to build relationships with others. Sports, art, travel, and religious activities are easy ways to build relationships and business networks. Finding activities that interest you and others disengage their defensive shields and allow you to share the same space with them. When the things you find important coincide with what they find important, rapport can often build easily and deeply. This can be true both personally and professionally.

Chapter 9

Flat Ass Rules

"State your flat-ass rules and stick to them. They shouldn't come as a surprise to anyone."–General "Mad Dog" James Mattis

"Flat Ass" Rules were created by General James Mattis during Operation Iraqi Freedom. These rules deal with three categories: pre/post-action strategies or planning, habits of thoughts, and finally, habits of action. One word stands out here, and that's the word *habits*.

What is a habit?

According to Dictionary.com, a habit is "an acquired behavior pattern regularly followed until it has become almost involuntary." This means that we learn these behaviors during our lives. Then we repeat them so many times that they become our norm – so normal to us that we don't even think about doing that particular behavior. We just automatically act in that same way when that same circumstance presents itself.

Most of our actions come from habitual behavior patterns that become automatic. This automatic behavior saves energy to help our brain process other stimuli and thoughts that it comes across on a daily basis. Habits can also constitute our internal rules for ourselves. These rules and habits dictate the thoughts we have, which can develop into opinions that control the actions we take on a daily basis. These actions are what give us the results we experience over time.

These habits and rules become our doctrines and beliefs. Whether right or wrong, these are the mottos that we live by. It seems that the older we get, the less likely we are to change these rules and habits. Why? Because over time, these rules and habits have given us certain results that provide evidence of their truth.

In today's society, we may believe in global warming and its destruction of our environment. We can find scientific evidence and media content supporting our beliefs. Because of this belief, we behave in ways that support our beliefs. We buy recyclable items. We drive electric cars. We sort through our trash and recycle the items that we can. We watch our use of certain resources to lower our carbon footprints. We donate to charities that follow our beliefs in helping our planet. We volunteer our time cleaning our community park. We do everything in our power to support our beliefs.

But what about the people that believe the opposite? They, too, can find media content supporting the belief that global warming doesn't exist and that it's a bunch of rubbish. Their belief forms their actions on how they live their lives. They shy away from recyclable items because they cost more money. They drive gas cars. They don't support charities that help global warming efforts, and they certainly don't volunteer their time cleaning their communities.

Who is right and who is wrong here? In reality, no one is wrong; they just have different beliefs and doctrines they live by. There's good and bad in every belief, but without beliefs, we humans would roam around without purpose.

Like General Mattis, this chapter will be organized into three parts:

- Planning
- Habits of Thought
- Habits of Action

This chapter will list a set of rules or beliefs that you can adopt (or not) to help guide you through life's twists and turns. These aren't necessarily all the rules I live by, but you'll understand later that these rules have been documented to do one thing: to make you think.

Then something new enters our awareness, we can either pay attention to it or let it go. Either way, we're aware of it, we've pondered it, and we've made a decision whether to incorporate it into our thoughts and actions or dismiss it. From then on, we can live according to our own "Flat Ass" rules.

The rest of this chapter dives into ideas from which you can create your own "Flat Ass" rules. This list is not all-encompassing. It may leave out things that are important to you. It may dwell on the same idea repeatedly. These are some ideas that I have observed throughout my life. Yours could differ depending on your age, background, environment, culture, or religion. That's okay. That's great. Take this list and mold it into what you can incorporate into your life to build something worthwhile.

Planning

"He who fails to plan is planning to fail."– Benjamin Franklin

1. How to Buy a House. Brian Preston from *The Money Guy* Podcast is a financial planner who has some rules on this topic to help his clients stay on track to be financially sound throughout their life and build wealth into retirement. Dave Ramsey, a radio personality and entrepreneur, has also helped millions of people get out of debt and build wealth and has similar rules for buying a house. 20% down. 15-year mortgage. The monthly payment cannot exceed 25% of your take-home pay. Of course, even better if you can buy cash for a house. But these are strategies all of us can use to keep our financial sheets balanced and strong. This 25% includes property taxes, HOA fees, and insurance. Dave Ramsey follows the same principles but also includes paying cash for the closing costs instead of rolling them into your mortgage loan, which can cost 3-4% of the purchase price. Dave also suggests getting preapproved for the loan prior to house hunting.

2. How to Buy a Car. Dave Ramsey differs from Brian Preston on this subject. Dave Ramsey wants you to buy the car in cash. No payments. Preferably a used car at least 4 years old, whereas a big chunk of the depreciation has already been set in the price. Brian Preston lays out the 20/3/8 plan. 20% down. Finance for no more than 3 years or 36 months. No more than 8% of your take-home pay. And 8% includes two cars if you're financing a car for your spouse or significant other. There's no leasing. Brian also wants luxury brands to be treated differently. If you can afford a luxury brand, you can afford to pay it off in 12 months instead of 36.

3. How much to save. Most financial schools of thought say three to six months of income should be saved. Dave Ramsey's baby steps state to save $1,000 as a starter emergency fund until all consumer debts- credit cards, student loans, and car payments excluding the house, are paid off. After paying off the consumer debt, a three to six months emergency fund can be saved. Where should this be saved? In a high-interest savings account. You want this money to be liquid and available in case something goes wrong, and you need to get it. You don't want to invest in it. Think of it as insurance for your emergency that will happen in the future.

4. Monthly Budget. Always have a budget. You can use Dave Ramsey's *Every Dollar* app (it's free.) Or you can create a spreadsheet. As long as you track your monthly expenses and income, you'll know exactly where all your money is going. A budget doesn't restrict you; it's controlled by you. All it does is tell your money where to go. It helps to keep us on track toward our financial and retirement goals. If we can track our progress, we can see how we're doing and adjust accordingly. I used the app and found money that never had the purpose of helping pay off my house early!

5. Daily To-Do List. Every day, record your personal and professional goals. Then write three actions you will take on each of these categories to move you closer to your goals. This needs to be on a physical piece of paper or in a journal so you can physically cross things off your list. By crossing things off your physical list, you've brought your non-physical thoughts into the physical world and taken action on them to create results. This is how targets and goals are met.

6. Backward Rule. I talk about this rule in my book, *The Backward Rule- The Ultimate Way to Hit Any Target.* Quantify your goal. Set a time limit. Work backward from there by defining the steps you will need to take to hit that target.

7. Save 40%. Most people don't make enough money to survive, let alone save 40% of their income. This means only one thing: you need to make more money. Depending on where you live, you can get your income to the point where you can live off the 20% left over after taxes are taken out. This 40% is then used to build an emergency fund of three to six months and then invest for retirement. You can reach any goal you set your mind to if you save 40% of your income.

8. Meal prep. Make a grocery list of ingredients you need to make a week's worth of meals. School lunches. Breakfasts. On-the-go items. Dinners. On the weekends, prepare the meals needed for the week and portion them out. If you have children in sports and activities, they can pick out a meal and take it with them. This cuts down on waste and take-out, which saves carbs and money.

9. Vitamins and supplements. Let your doctor do blood lab work to see what vitamins and minerals you lack. Maybe you need some probiotics. Maybe calcium. Maybe Vitamin D3. Unless your blood is tested, you won't know what's lacking and what amount is needed to optimize your body.

10. Date night with honey. Plan a weekly date night with your honey where you can create communication and intimacy. This is where you plan your life together. This is where you dream together. This is where you become a team.

11. "Me" time. Set aside at least 30 minutes every day for alone time. Use this time to meditate, take a walk, and work out. Use this time to work on yourself, your goals, and your dreams. Everyone deserves time to themselves. Put the kids to bed or ask your honey to help and get away to ponder life's issues and solutions.

12. Control resources. Money. Time. Energy. These are the only resources that you can control. Budget. Make a 'To-Do List.' Eat a low-carbohydrate diet. Use your resources to reach success for you and not for someone else. Stop giving other people your resources.

13. Invest early. Brian Preston from *The Money Guy* podcast calculated that every dollar you invest when you're 20 can be worth 88 times that amount by the time you're 65. It's called compound growth. Money makes money, and then that money also makes money. Like a tree with branches that grow outward, money can do that too if you give it enough time to do its job. Multiply. The sooner you start, the more it will grow.

14. Protect your body. While exercising, wrap your knees, back, and ankles. Avoid contact sports where injuries can occur and can be permanent. If a joint has a previous injury, protect it with a shield or wrap. Wear eye and ear protection while around dangerous and noisy machinery. You only get one body; protect it.

15. Shop prices. Use coupons. Shop the sales. Compare prices at different outlets. Buy used goods and cars. Get the biggest bang for your buck by being frugal with your dollars and cents.

16. Will. Everyone should have a will, a power of attorney, a health directive, and a living trust. These documents tell your loved ones where you want your belongings to go, your organs, and your money if you die before them. Do you want a judge to determine who gets what? Then these documents are vital to providing you and your family peace of mind.

17. Be early. Wake up early. Be prepared for the deadline early. Show up to your meeting early. Being early creates enthusiasm and urgency in all that you do. It's respectful of your time and those around you. It's unprofessional and not polite to show up late. There's no such thing as *fashionably late*. Those that show up early are present and ready to win.

18. Eliminate impulse. Impulse buying can lead to credit card debt. Impulse eating can lead to obesity and diabetes. Impulse speaking can lead to losing your job. Only emergencies need to have impulse action and thought. Everything else can be pondered over. Do your research and check your budget before you make any rash decisions. Your future self will thank you.

19. Carpe Diem. Seize the day. Plan your day out. Create goals and then take action to hit them. Spend deliberate time on your own health and mental wellness as well as your family's. Live as much today as you can with focus, energy, love, intention, and fun.

20. Minimize payments. When you accept a payment plan, you create a bond with that debt that will last for months to years. This bond promises future earnings will go from your bank account to theirs. Is that commitment worth it? By delaying gratification until the money is saved, the future commitment is to your bank account, not theirs.

21. Moderation. Everything in moderation. Enjoy life without going to extremes. Plan healthy balanced meals. Take time for yourself. Workout. Notch out a little honey time. A little bit here and there can help maintain balance and happiness without leaving your potential.

Habits of Thought

"Change your habits, change your life!"–
Stephanie Aldrich

---

1. **Continue to learn.** Be a lifelong student. I *practice* dentistry every day. Not every situation is taught in a textbook. We need experience and trial and error to see what works. We need to know when this works and when this doesn't work. This all comes from experience and the continuation of exploring and learning new ideas and implementing them.

2. **The Law of Polarity.** Everything has an equal and opposite. When we say "no" to something, we simultaneously say "yes" to something else. When we spend our money on this, we can't necessarily spend our money on that.

3. **The 90% Rule.** In *Essentialism by* Greg McKeown, he explains the 90% rule. It's either a "hell yes," or it's automatically a "no." There's no in-between. You either love it or you don't. You either will do it or you won't. This task will either take you toward your goal or won't. To be productive and efficient, we must ask ourselves if it's

essential or not. Is it a must? Is it 100% necessary? If so, go for it.

4. Finish 100%. If you start a project, ensure you allow enough time and resources to finish it and clean up the mess afterward. This includes professional projects as well.

5. Do your best. No matter how big or small the task is, ask yourself, "Did I do this to the best of my ability?" How we do one thing is how we do everything, no matter how simple or complex.

6. Buy quality over quantity. If an item is made well, it will last longer. Living with intention doesn't mean living as a cheap miser. Buying quality allows you to spend money on other things. You won't have to replace that item as often or repair it. Buying quality is an investment, not a lost cost.

7. Replace or upgrade when broken or obsolete. There's always going to be an upgrade or improvement. The entire marketing and advertising industry feeds on our desires for shiny new objects. Resist the urge to spend your hard-earned dollars on every new item released to the market. Only replace objects like clothes or electronics when they are broken/torn or obsolete. Think of how much money you can save and invest for the future if you're not wasting it on upgrades today.

8. Don't make excuses. Unsuccessful people make excuses. They blame everyone and everything for the lack of success they experience. Don't be one of those people. Take responsibility for your life. The only person to blame for your situation is the one staring at you in the mirror.

9. Partner with people. Partner with people that have different skills than you. No one is good at everything. Build on your strengths and allow others to fill in the gaps with theirs.

10. Record ideas. We all can record our voices or notes on our phones. If you're in the middle of a project or need to brainstorm, keep your phone handy when ideas pop up. You never know when a breakthrough will occur.

11. How can I? Don't say, "I can't." Ask yourself to start thinking of ways to solve the problem or pay for the desired item. "How can I?" This question opens your thought faculties to research possibilities of making it happen. Is it possible? Are other people experiencing this thing or situation that I want? If so, find a way to make it happen for you.

12. Learn another language. It's fun. It's difficult. It illuminates parts of our brains that we don't always use. And if we go on vacation, we can use their native language and communicate easier with the locals.

13. Lower expectations. You can never be disappointed if you don't expect something from someone. Expect nothing but the best from yourself and your performance, but lower your expectations for others as others may not live up to the hype.

14. Mentors. Hire mentoring from others that have what you want. Hire trainers that can help you get the results you want. This will take out time and a lot of frustration throwing up ideas and taking actions that don't work. Bypass the frustration by learning methods that work from people who have already figured it all out.

15. Have fun. Be silly. Joke and laugh. Life doesn't always have to be serious or dire. Make things fun and enjoy life's little moments. Build a memory from dancing and singing together with friends and loved ones.

16. Enjoy music and art. Surround yourself with the expression and wonder of art and music. Allow your mind to relax and enjoy the creativity of the artists.

17. Simplify. Live simply. Talk simply. Break down complex issues into simple steps that anyone can follow. Obligations, payments, and processed foods use the energy needed to live a happy, productive life. Downgrade. Minimize. Simplify. Then you can relax and have fun.

18. Fundamentals. Learn them and become a master. Professional athletes practice their fundamentals every day. They perform them at optimal levels.

19. Moderation. Have fun, but not too much. Be serious, but not too serious. Eat your favorite food, but not every day. Drink a little. Buy yourself something special, but not every day. Everything in moderation. As my friend Lara says, "Make it epic, but not too epic!"

20. Find out for yourself. Don't allow friends, social media, or traditional media to sway your opinions about life and social issues. Find out for yourself. Read. Ask questions. Get answers. Learn the truth and then make up your mind after you know the facts. Trust but verify.

21. Avoid the news. Media content is not what it used to be. Now all content is someone's opinion on the news. It's not the facts about what's happening in the world around us. That's a shame, but that's where we are right now.

Avoid the opinion makers and learn about the world through history and experience. Not the mass media.

22. Don't quit. You may need to change directions, but don't change directions until you've exhausted every possible method of reaching your goal in front of you. Don't quit until you succeed. The old saying goes, "Winners never quit, and quitters never win."

23. Network. They say that "network is your net worth." People buy products and services. The more people you know, the more opportunities you have to get your product or service into their hands. Meet people and keep their contacts. You never know who may help you with a future opportunity.

24. Celebrate. When we have a win, a birthday, or a special occasion, celebrate! That doesn't mean going crazy, spending tons of money, or binging on food and drink. It means to make it a big deal. Create a buzz. Have fun and create pride in yourself that you accomplished your goal. Make sure it includes cake! ;)

25. Build on strengths. Don't waste time working on your weaknesses. You can surround yourself with others who excel in the areas where you're weak. Develop and accelerate your strengths and reap the rewards.

26. Be handy. It doesn't take a rocket scientist to replace a broken switch, fix your sink, or paint your wall. Sometimes the jobs are too difficult for an amateur, but nine out of ten, the job is at the amateur's skill level. Nowadays, there are *How To* videos all over the internet where you can learn how to fix something. Learning to be handy saves a ton of money and strengthens your character, knowing that you can fix things when they go wrong. And when you own anything, things definitely will go wrong. Pick and choose and learn to be handy.

27. Be present. There's a saying by Eckhart Tolle that says, "The more you are focused on time — past and future — the more you miss the *Now*, the most precious thing there is." Live intentionally with the now. It's the only time you're guaranteed. Have fun with your family. Enjoy the seasonal, cultural, and community festivities and activities that occur. Build memories that will last a lifetime. There's no better time than now.

28. Minimize fast food. This goes without saying that fast food is bad for you. It's loaded with chemicals and trans fat that your body can't use to do its thing. Learn to cook and feed yourself and your family nutritious food.

29. Be nice. Be nice to everyone. Service people. Customers. Neighbors. Family members. Even people that you don't like or are mean and rude to you. Their behavior says enough about them, while yours says enough about you. Treat everyone like you want to be treated and be respectful and helpful. The Golden Rule.

30. Don't be busy. Busy people aren't necessarily productive or efficient people. To be productive, you must know what is essential and what isn't. *Efficiency* comes from getting the job done in less time and with less energy. *Busy* usually means focusing your attention on mundane tasks. *Productive*, on the other hand, creates a goal and then hits it. It's a more intentional use of resources.

31. Decrease dead time. Robert Greene, author of *The 48 Laws of Power,* described dead time versus alive time. *Dead time* is when we are passive and waiting for something to happen, while *alive time* is when we are learning, active, and utilizing every second. Eliminate passivity and take some action. That's the only way to reach your goals.

32. Love the process. The goal is not to reach it but to become a better person along the way. Fall in love with the process of learning and becoming a better you.

33. Get out of your comfort zone. You can't learn anything new unless you try something new. You will fail.

You will be lousy at it. It's okay. Everyone is lousy when they first do something new. Love the process, and keep trying. You will eventually get it and improve your skills.

34. Admiration. Don't get caught up in achievement and admiration. Do things because they are right and to the best of your ability. People will build you up just as quickly as they tear you down. Create a thick skin on criticism, and don't get too high with admiration or too low with critiques.

35. Know what matters. What's important? Family? A successful career? A healthy, loving relationship? A toned, healthy body? Schedule your day to reflect on what's important to you and what matters. In the end, you'll live the life you've always wanted because those intentional moments all add up.

36. **Be humble.** You don't have to try to make yourself important to others. You know deep inside what you are worth. There's no need to boast or project your importance onto others. Live with humility and pride; others will feel your strength and be drawn to it.

Habits of Action

"Do you want to know who you are? Don't ask. Act! Action will delineate and define you." – Thomas Jefferson

1. Daily exercise. If something is good to do, it's good to do every day. Only half of Americans exercise three times a week, according to HealthyLiving.azcentral.com. Even if it's a simple 30-minute walk, moving our bodies helps to decrease blood pressure, heart disease, and cancer. We can increase our strength, flexibility, and endurance by using our muscles. When in doubt, move.

2. Intermittent Fasting. Dave Asprey wrote the bible on Intermittent fasting called *Fast This Way*. I highly recommend reading this book. Our bodies need time to get the toxins and dead cells removed. If we're constantly eating, our body needs to use its resources for digestion instead of detoxification. Fasting 12-16 hours per day will give our bodies enough time to remove inflammation, toxins, and cellular by-products.

3. Pay in cash. The movies. A restaurant. Anything small, pay in cash. This helps to keep you on your budget. If you only have $20 to spend, you can't go over if you only have a $20 bill.

4. Envelope system. My mother taught me how to use the envelope system. After doing your budget, you will set aside a certain amount of cash that will be saved and used for something. A vacation. A new sweeper. Shoes for the kids. Once you've saved enough cash, you can buy the item you've saved for. This way, you're not ruining your budget by buying things on impulse. If you must save for three months, you will know in your heart that it's necessary and you're not wasting your money on something that you don't want or need.

5. Treat yourself once a week. Everyone needs to enjoy life. If you're strict with your diet (and you should be) and you do intermittent fasting, it's good for your body to reset and not get into a rhythmic continuation of the same routine each day. Make a huge breakfast on Saturday. Have a drink or two with some friends after work. Make some popcorn and make tonight a movie night, and just chill. The problem with most Americans is we treat ourselves every day. There's no discipline or self-control in our impulses and pleasures, which explains our financial, mental, and bodily stresses.

6. Read one new book a week. This book isn't a fiction fairy tale. This book should include topics such as business, philosophy, or mindset. This will help you learn new ways to cope with stress and build leadership skills that everyone can improve. The average American reads four books a year, lives paycheck to paycheck, and is overweight. Coincidence? Success can be learned through reading.

7. Buy in bulk. Meats and non-perishable items in particular. Buy a Foodsaver. Grill all of your meats. Allow them to cool. Divide them into portions and use the Foodsaver to vacuum-seal the packages and freeze them for another day. It will last a year without freezer burn.

8. Ask questions. How will you know unless you ask? Don't be ashamed or fearful. If you don't know how to do something, ask someone who does so you can learn. If you're not sure, ask someone who is sure. Breakthroughs don't occur without asking questions.

9. Use simple language. Most people communicate on a 5th grade level. If you have technical training, only speak technically when talking to other professionals. If you're connecting with the public, those who aren't trained in your industry, use simple language, so your clients understand what you're saying. You will make more sales and gain repeat customers if they know they can rely on you to solve their problems.

10. Be a great conversationalist. How? Ask the other person about themselves. Everyone loves to talk about themselves and what's going on in their lives. Want to gain a client? Ask them about the problems they are experiencing at work. Then let them know how your product or service can solve their problems.

11. Listen. Hearing someone and listening to them are two different things. Hearing is a physical sense that involves your ears, nerves, and brain. Listening involves your brain and understanding what the other person is trying to communicate to you. If you want to be successful, listen.

12. Use manners. It's a matter of respect. A *please* and *thank you* can go a long way. Help those that are older than you. Use *Ma'am, Sir, Mister, or Misses*.

13. Digitize everything. We still live in a paper society, somewhat. If you have old baby pictures, scan them. If you have paper tax returns or receipts, scan them. Anything that's paper, scan it and back it up in a cloud service.

14. Eat low-carb. Keto or paleo diets can help to keep you fit and healthy. Weight Watchers can help to keep your carbohydrate and calorie loads within normal limits. The more carbs you eat, the higher chance you'll store them as fat, and the weight will pour on. Decrease simple sugars and starchy foods, and the carb count will stay under control. Keto incorporates higher fatty foods, which decrease appetite and is more difficult to break down.

15. Wear sunscreen. Over 100,000 new cases of melanoma occur every year in America. After a couple of hours, reapply. If swimming or exercising, reapply more often.

16. Buy investments that generate income. These can include dividend-paying index funds, businesses, oil, advertising campaigns, forex trading bots, and real estate. That's what wealthy people do. They invest in strategies that make them more money. Money multiplies money.

17. Buy a hot tub. If you're over 40, invest in a hot tub. The jets will beat that water on your achy back and joints, and it will help keep you flexible and strong.

18. Cook. It will save money and carbohydrates. It's fun and an easy way to connect with friends and family. Make it a tradition to enjoy a homemade meal with your family at least once a week. Treat that meal as a connection meal. Talk about your lives and connect with one another.

19. Be the cause. Don't wait for something to happen or to change. Take action and cause it to happen. Then you're not waiting around for a day that will never come. Remember that no one will come to save you. Take action to save yourself.

20. Travel. Experience new places and cultures. Learn their languages. Eat their food. Allow other worlds to penetrate your heart and your psyche. And, of course, take lots of photos and videos along the way to remind yourself and others of where you've been.

21. Buy local. Support the small businesses in your community by purchasing their services and products. This helps keep the economy strong and flowing near your home.

22. Learn martial arts. Everyone has the right to defend themselves against an attack. However, not everyone knows how to do this. Take a self-defense course or a mixed martial art to help protect you and your loved ones.

23. Pursuing hobbies. Paint. Write. Golf. Run. Do something involving your body and mind that helps you relax and use your innate creativity. You don't have to be great at it; just enjoy doing it and find time to pursue it.

24. See a functional medicine doctor. Functional medicine is a branch of medicine that concentrates on optimal functioning. They look at everything from hormones to vitamins and minerals. They know how you're supposed to work and what results you're getting. They know how to tweak medications and supplements to feel good and live with abundant energy.

25. Eliminate social media. The average American consumes four hours of social media daily. If you have a small business, use social media to expand your brand and marketing efforts. If not, spend your time reading, enjoying your family, or exploring your hobbies. Eliminate the time suck that social media has become.

26. Keep up with the Joneses. Who are these people, and why do we care about them? Stop comparing yourself and what you have with other people. If you want to live a successful and fulfilled life, that means you're doing what you want to do. That doesn't involve anyone else and what they have that you don't. Ignore what your friends have and focus on what you want and how you will get it.

27. Maintenance. Keep up with repairs and maintenance on things that you own; this includes your body. Make sure you make regular appointments with the doctor, dentist, and chiropractor to keep your body strong. Rotate your tires and change the oil. Paint things that need to be painted. Get the furnace and air conditioner checked. Maintaining something is cheaper and easier than replacing it.

28. Drink water. We drink so many things containing artificial ingredients, sweeteners, and caffeine. Our bodies are made from 90% water. Replenish what your body needs by drinking water every day. Yes, plain, dull water. Your body needs it.

29. Pack your lunch. I know going out with friends or colleagues for lunch is fun. But let's face it, it can get rather expensive. Packing your lunch saves time and money that can be better spent on paying debt and building wealth. It also is healthier because you're controlling the ingredients, not someone else.

30. Floss every day. 46% of the cavities I fill in my office are between teeth. The food that's wedged in that area can easily be removed by flossing. Floss before you go to bed to decrease the time and money you spend at the dentist.

31. Eat something green. Eat some veggies daily to give your body the necessary nutrients to stay healthy and rebuild itself properly. You'll increase your energy, feel better, and rest in the fact that you're doing all you can to keep your body healthy and strong.

32. Make a shopping list. If you make a list, you will be better prepared during your shopping trip and less likely to buy things you won't eat or don't need. A list helps you stick to your budget. A list helps you stick to your eating plan. A list saves time so you can quickly get in and out of the grocery store.

33. Use the library. There's a place where you can get audiobooks, written books, videos, movies, and magazines for free. It's called your local library. There's an app called Libby where you link your library card number to the online library community and access all the digital content out there. It's amazing, and it's free! Don't waste your money buying books or magazine subscriptions. Use Libby and gain knowledge free in the comfort of your home or office.

34. Follow up. Anything worth having is worth pursuing. If you want to hit your professional goals, follow up with customers. If you want to hit your personal goals, revisit them several times a day and record your progress. Ask a question and get an answer. Meet new people and make sure they know you can solve their problems with your products and services. If you don't follow up, they may think you don't care about them and their wants and needs. Hence, follow up without being creepy!

35. Clean underwear. Always shower, shave, and put on clean underwear. You never know when something might happen- good or bad, and someone else will be seeing your undies! Hot date? Groom and lay a foundation for an awesome adventure. Bike ride in the woods? Groom before you go should you need a quick trip to the emergency room. Not enough time to take a shower for an after-work event? Grab a clean pair of undies to keep you feeling fresh all night long.

36. Work hard. Always do your best. Go to work early, and stay at work longer than anyone else. No one is going to give it to you. If you want it, you're going to have to go after it which means you have to be better than the competition. No one died from working hard. The wealthiest people on Earth still work hard every day. Find your strengths and be the best!

About the Author

Stephanie Aldrich is a general dentist, speaker, trainer, entrepreneur, and author of five other books and programs, including *There's No Crying in the Man's World, Nothing But the Tooth: 11 Question You Should Ask Your Dentist, The Habit Formula: Life's Success Equation, The Habit Formula: A Parent's Success Equation Kid's Edition*, and *The Backward Rule: The Ultimate Way to Hit Any Target.*

Coming from humble beginnings in a small town in Ohio, Dr. Aldrich continues to strive for success for not only herself and her companies but also for others. Knowing that anything is possible drives her creativity to handle issues plaguing individuals and companies. When you start with the individual and what's in it for them, you can implement change that trickles down to the company as a whole.

Dr. Aldrich lives in Copley, Ohio, with her loving husband, Steven, and their wonderful son, Noah.

www.ingramcontent.com/pod-product-compliance
Lightning Source LLC
LaVergne TN
LVHW051458080426
835509LV00017B/1806